Gold Dust

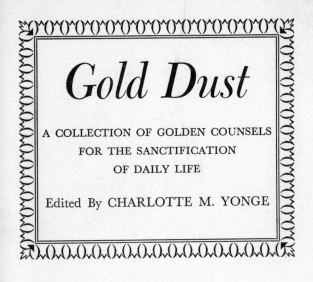

Gold Dust

A COLLECTION OF GOLDEN COUNSELS
FOR THE SANCTIFICATION
OF DAILY LIFE

Edited By CHARLOTTE M. YONGE

PUBLISHERS

Grosset & Dunlap

NEW YORK

Printed in the United States of America

To

E. B .H.

This little book is most lovingly dedicated

PREFACE

THIS little book is a translation
from a collection of devotional
thoughts published in France under
the title of "Paillettes d'Or." It is
necessarily a selection, since the gold
dust which suits French readers requires a fresh sifting for the English;
but the value of most of the thoughts
seems to me well to deserve the term
of gold. There are many who will
much enjoy having this little collection on their table, so as to be able to
take it up and dwell upon some one
of its grains at leisure times throughout the day's business.

C. M. YONGE.

Feb. 12, 1880.

INTRODUCTION

IN the south of France, during the summer, little children and old and infirm poor who are incapable of hard work, in order to earn a livelihood, employ themselves in searching the beds of dried up rivers for "Paillettes d'Or," or golden dust, which sparkles in the sun, and which the water carries away as it flows. What is done by these poor people and little children for the gold dust GOD has sown in those obscure rivers, we would do with those counsels and teachings which GOD has sown almost everywhere, which sparkle, enlighten, and inspire for a moment, then disappear, leaving but regret that the thought

did not occur to collect and treasure
them.

Who is there that has not experienced at some time in his life those
teachings so soft and gentle, yet so
forcible, which make the heart thrill,
and reveal to it suddenly a world of
peace, joy, and devotion?

It may have been but a word read
in a book, or a sentence overheard in
conversation, which may have had for
us a two-fold meaning, and, in passing, left us touched with an unknown
power.

It was the smile on the lips of a
beloved one whom we knew to be
sorrowful, that spoke to us of the
sweet joy of resignation.

It was the open look of an innocent
child that revealed to us all the beauty
of frankness and simplicity.

Oh! if we had but treasured all the
rays of light that cross our path and
sparkle but for a moment; oh! if we

had but engraved them on our hearts!
what a guide and comfort they would
have been to us in the days of discouragement and sorrow; what counsels to
guide our actions, what consolations
to soothe the broken heart!

How many new means of doing
good!

It is this simple work of gathering a
little from every source—from nature,
from books, above all, from mankind
itself—that is the intention of one of
your fellow-creatures, dear souls, you
who long so to make your lives more
holy and devout!

And in the same way as the gold
dust, gathered and accumulated from
the river's bed, was the means of
bringing a little profit to the hearth, so
would we endeavor to carry a little
joy to your hearts, and peace to your
souls.

Gather, then, these little counsels;
gather them with watchfulness; let

them for a moment penetrate deep into your heart; then scatter them abroad again, that they may go with their good words to the help of others.

They will not be importunate, will not even ask to be preserved; they do not desire fame; all that they seek is to convey a transient blessing.

GOLD DUST

I.

"MY LORD!" exclaimed once a devout soul, "give me every day a little work to occupy my mind; a little suffering to sanctify my spirit; a little good to do to comfort my heart."

II.

IF by our deeds we become saints, true it is, that by our deeds also we shall be condemned.

Yes, it is little by little that we press onward, either towards salvation or eternal ruin; and when at last

15

we reach the gate of glory, or that of
perdition, the cry escapes our lips,
"Already!"

The first backward step is almost
imperceptible; it was those tiny flakes
of snow, seeming to melt as they touch
the earth, but falling one upon another,
that have formed that immense mass
which seems ready to fall and crush us.

Ah! if I tried to trace back to what
first led to that act of sin, the thought
that produced the desire, the circum-
stance that gave rise to the thought, I
should find something almost imperceptible; perhaps a word with a *double
entendre* I had heard, and at which
I had smiled; a useless explanation,
sought out of mere curiosity; a hasty
look, cast I knew not wherefore, and
which conscience prompted me to
check; a prayer neglected, because it
wearied me; work left undone, while
I indulged in some day-dream that
flitted before my fancy. . . .

A week later the same things occur, but this time more prolonged; the stifled voice of conscience is hushed.

Yet another week. . . . Alas! let us stop there; each can complete the sad story for himself, and it is easy to draw the practical conclusion.

III.

A YOUNG girl, in one of those moments when the heart seems to overflow with devotion, wrote thus in her journal: "If I dared, I would ask GOD why I am placed in the world; what have I to do? I know not; my days are idly spent, and I do not even regret them. . . . If I might but do some good to myself or another, if only for the short space of a minute in each day!" A few days later, when in a calmer mood she re-read these lines, she added, "Why, nothing is easier! I have but to give a cup of cold water to one of CHRIST's little ones."

Even *less* than that: a word of advice; something lent to another; a little vexation patiently borne; a prayer for a friend offered to GOD; the fault or thoughtlessness of another repaired without his knowledge—GOD will recompense it all a thousand-fold!

IV.

ALMS given in secret; that is the charity which brings a blessing.

What sweet enjoyment to be able to shed a little happiness around us!

What an easy and agreeable task is that of trying to render others happy.

FATHER! if I try to please and imitate Thee thus, wilt Thou indeed bless me? Thanks! thanks! be unto Thee.

V.

IS it fair always to forget all the good or kindness shown to us by those with whom we live, for the sake of *one* little pain they may have caused us, and which, most likely, was quite unintentional on their part?

VI.

WHEN you sometimes find in books advice or example that you think may be of service, you take care to copy and consult it as an oracle. Do as much for the good of your soul. Engrave in your memory, and even write down, the counsels and precepts that you hear or read; . . . then, from time to time, study this little collection, which you will not prize the less that you have made it all yourself.

Books written by others in time become wearisome to us, but of those we write ourselves we never tire. And it *will* be yours, this collection of thoughts chosen because you liked them; counsels you have given yourself; moral receipts you have discovered, and of which, perhaps, you have proved the efficacy.

Happy soul! that each day reaps its harvest.

VII.

DO you wish to live at peace with all the world? Then practise the maxims of an influential man, who, when asked, after the Revolution, how he managed to escape the executioner's axe, replied, "I made myself of no reputation and kept silence."

Would you live peaceably with the members of your family, above all with those who exercise a certain control of you? Use the means employed by a pious woman, who had to live with one of a trying temper, and which she summed up in the following words:—

"I do everything to please her.

"I fulfil all my duties with a smiling face, never revealing the trouble it causes me.

"I bear patiently everything that displeases me.

"I consult her on many subjects of which, perhaps, I may be the better judge."

Would you be at peace with your conscience? Let your Guardian Angel find you at each moment of the day doing one of these four things which once formed the rule of a saintly life: (1.) praying; (2.) laboring; (3.) striving after holiness; (4.) practising patience.

Would you become holy? Try to add to the above actions the following virtues: method, faith, spiritual combat, perseverance.

Finally, if you would live in an atmosphere of benevolence, make it your study to be always rendering others service, and never hesitate to ask the same of them.

In offering help, you make a step towards gaining a friend; in asking it, you please by this mark of your confidence. The result of this will be a constant habit of mutual forbearance, and a fear to be disobliging in matters of greater importance.

VIII.

WHEN teaching or working with others, never laugh or make fun of their awkwardness. If it is caused by stupidity, your laughter is uncharitable; if from ignorance, your mockery is, to say the least, unjust.

Teach the unskilful with gentleness; show him the right way to work; and GOD, Who sees all your efforts, will smile on your patience, and send you help in all your difficulties.

IX.

WHEN the heart is heavy, and we suffer from depression or disappointment, how thankful we should be that we still have work and prayer left to comfort us. Occupation forcibly diverts the mind; prayer sweetly soothes the soul.

"Then," writes one who had been sorely tried, "I tell my griefs to GOD, as a child tells its troubles to its mother; and when I have told all I am comforted, and repeat with a lightened heart the prayer of S. Françoise de Chantal (who certainly suffered more than I), 'Thy will be done for ever and ever, O LORD, without *if* or *but;'* . . . and then, for fear a murmur may arise in my heart, I return immediately to my work, and become absorbed in occupation."

X.

HE who is never satisfied with anything, satisfies no one.

XI.

ARE there many who try to be of some little help or comfort to the souls with whom they are brought in contact through life?

Poor souls, that, perhaps, have no longer strength or will to manifest the longing they experience, and who languish for want of help, without being aware that they are perishing. Oh, mingle sometimes with your earthly help the blessed Name of GOD; and if there remain one little spark of life in the soul, that Name will rekindle it, and carry comfort and resignation; even as air breathed into the mouth of any one apparently dead, rushes into the lungs, and revives the sufferer, if but one breath of life remains.

Souls! Souls! I yearn for Souls!
—This is the cry of the SAVIOUR; and
for their sakes He died upon the Cross,
and remains until eternity their Inter-
cessor.

Souls! Souls! I must win Souls!
—It is the cry of Satan; and to obtain
them he scatters gold to tempt them,
multiplies their pleasures and vanities,
and gives the praise that only in-
fatuates.

Souls! Souls! we long for Souls!
—Let this be our aim, readers and
writers of these our "Paillettes;" and
for the sake of even *one* soul, let not
fatigue, expense, or the criticism of
the world, deter us. . . .

XII.

HOW few there are who would thus
dare to address GOD each night:
"LORD, deal with me to-morrow as I
have this day dealt with others; . . .

those to whom I was harsh, and from
malice, or to show my own superiority,
exposed their failings; others, to
whom, from pride or dislike, I refused
to speak,—one I have avoided, another
I cannot like because she displeases
me; I will not forgive,—to whom I
will not show any kindness." . . .

And yet let us never forget that,
sooner or later, GOD will do unto us
even as we have done unto them.

XIII.

"GRANT me, O LORD," said a
humble soul, "that I may pass
unnoticed through the world."

This should be the wish, or rather
the aim, of all true devotion.

Small virtues require the praise of
man to sustain them, just as little children require encouragement to walk
or stand alone.

But true virtue goes quietly through

the world, scattering good around, and performing noble deeds, without even the knowledge that what it does is heroic.

XIV.

S. CHANTAL one day was excusing herself to S. François de Sales for having spoken hastily to some one, on the plea that it was in the cause of justice. The Saint replied, "You have been more just than righteous; but we should be more righteous than just."

XV.

A DEVOUT woman once wrote thus: "In my own family I try to be as little in the way as possible, satisfied with everything, and never to believe for a moment that any one means unkindly towards me.

"If people are friendly and kind to me, I enjoy it; if they neglect me, or leave me, I am always happy alone. It all tends to my one aim, forgetfulness of self in order to please GOD."

XVI.

LEARNING is not without its effect upon the soul; it either lends it wings to bear it up to GOD, or leaves behind it tiny sparks, which little by little consume the whole being.

If you would ascertain all the good or ill you have derived from all those hours devoted to historians, poets, novelists, or philosophers, put to yourself these questions: Since acquiring this knowledge, am I wiser? am I better? am I happier?

Wiser?—That is to say, more self-controlled, less the slave of my passions, less irritated by small vexations, braver in bearing misfortunes, more careful to live for eternity?

Better?—More forbearing towards

others, more forgiving, less uncharitable, more reticent in opposing the
faults of others, more solicitous for the
happiness of those around me?

Happier?—That would mean more
contented with my station in life, striving to derive all possible benefits from
it, to beautify rather than to alter it?

Have I more faith in GOD, and more
calmness and resignation in all the
events of life?

If you cannot reply in the affirma-
tive, then examine your heart thor-
oughly, and you will find there, stifling
the good that GOD has implanted, these
three tyrants that have obtained dominion over you: (1.) Pride; (2.)
Ambition; (3.) Self-conceit.

From them have sprung: dissatis-
faction and contempt of your life and
its surroundings, restlessness, a longing for power and dominion over
others, malice, habitual discontent, and
incessant murmurings. Have you any

further doubts? Then inquire of those with whom you live.

Ah! if this be indeed the sad result, then, whatever may be your age, close, oh! close those books, and seek once more those two elements of happiness you ought never to have forsaken, and which, had you made them the companions of your study, would have kept you pure and good.

I refer to prayer and manual labor.

XVII.

LISTEN to the story of a simple shepherd, given in his own words: "I forget now who it was that once said to me, 'Jean Baptiste, you are very poor?'—True.—'If you fell ill, your wife and children would be destitute?'—True. And then I felt anxious and uneasy for the rest of the day.

"At Evensong wiser thoughts came

to me, and I .said to myself: Jean
Baptiste, for more than thirty years
you have lived in the world, you have
never possessed anything, yet still you
live on, and have been provided each
day with nourishment, each night with
repose. Of trouble GOD has never sent
you more than your share. Of help
the means have never failed you. To
whom do you owe all this? To GOD.
Jean Baptiste, be no longer ungrateful,
and banish those anxious thoughts;
for what could ever induce you to
think that the Hand from which you
have already received so much, would
close against you when you grow old,
and have greater need of help? I
finished my prayer, and felt at peace."

XVIII.

THE work of the Sower is given to
each of us in this world, and we
fall short of our duty when we let

those with whom we are brought in contact leave us without having given them a kind thought or pious impression.

Nothing is so sad as the cry, "I am useless!" Happily none need ever *be* so.

A kind word, a gentle act, a modest demeanor, a loving smile, are as so many seeds that we can scatter every moment of our lives, and which will always spring up and bear fruit.

Happy are those who have many around them . . . they are rich in opportunities, and may sow plenteously.

XIX.

FEW positions in life are so full of importunities as that of the mother of a family, or mistress of a house. She may have a dozen interruptions while writing *one* letter, or settling an account. What holiness, what self-control, is needed to be always calm and unruffled amid these little vexations, and never to manifest the slightest impatience!

Leaving the work without apparent annoyance, replying with a smile upon the lips, awaiting patiently the end of a long conversation, and finally returning calmly to the yet unfinished work —all this is the sign of a recollected soul, and one that waits upon GOD.

Oh! what blessings are shed around them by such patient souls . . . but, alas! how rarely they are to be met with!

XX

THERE are times in one's life when all the world seems to turn against us. Our motives are misunderstood, our words misconstrued, a malicious smile or an unkind word reveals to us the unfriendly feelings of others. Our advances are repulsed, or

met with icy coldness; a dry refusal
arrests on our lips the offer of
help. . . .

Oh, how hard it all seems, and the
more so that we cannot divine the
cause!

Courage, patience, poor disconsolate
one! GOD is making a furrow in your
heart, where He will surely sow His
grace.

It is rare when injustice, or slights
patiently borne, do not leave the heart
at the close of the day filled with mar-
vellous joy and peace.

It is the seed GOD has sown, springing up and bearing fruit.

XXI.

THAT which costs little is of little
worth. This thought should
make us tremble. In our self-exami-
nation we may experience at times a
certain satisfaction in noticing the lit-

tle virtues we may possess, above all, those that render us pleasing in the eyes of others.

For instance, we may like to pray at a certain place, with certain sentiments, and we think ourselves devout; we are gentle, polite, and smiling towards one person in particular; patient with those we fear, or in whose good opinion we would stand; we are devoted, charitable, generous, because the heart experiences an unspeakable pleasure in spending and being spent for others; we suffer willingly at the hands of some one we love, and then say we are patient; we are silent, because we have no inclination to speak; shunning society because we fail to shine there, and then fancy that we love retirement.

Take these virtues that give you such self-satisfaction, one by one, and ask yourself at what sacrifice, labor, or cost, above all, with what care you

have managed to acquire them. . . .
Alas! you will find that all that patience, affability, generosity, and piety
are but as naught, springing from a
heart puffed up with pride. It costs
nothing, and it is worthless.

As self-sacrifice, says De Maistre, is
the basis and essence of virtue, so
those virtues are the most meritorious
that have cost the greatest effort to
attain.

Do not look with so much pride on
this collection of virtues, but rather
bring yourself to account for your
faults. Take just one, the first that
comes, impatience, sloth, gossip, un-
charitableness, sulkiness, whatever it
may be, and attack it bravely.

It will take at least a month, calcu-
lating upon three victories every day,
not indeed to eradicate it,—a fault is
not so short-lived,—but to prevent its
attaining dominion over you.

That one subdued, then take another. It is the work of a lifetime; and truly to our faults may we apply the saying, *"Quand il n'y en a plus, il y en a encore."*

"Happy should I think myself," said S. Francis de Sales, "if I could rid myself of my imperfections but *one-*quarter of an hour previous to my death."

XXII.

Before Holy Communion

JESUS

MY child, it is not wisdom *I* require of thee, it sufficeth if thou lovest Me well.

Speak to Me as thou wouldst talk to thy mother if she were here, pressing thee to her heart.

❋

Hast thou none for whom thou wouldst intercede? Tell Me the names of thy kindred and thy friends; and at the mention of each name add what thou wouldst have Me do for them. Ask much fervently; the generous hearts that forget themselves for others are very dear unto Me.

Tell Me of the poor thou wouldst succor, the sick thou hast seen suffering, the sinful thou wouldst reclaim, the estranged thou wouldst receive to thy heart again.

Pray fervently for all mankind.

Remind Me of My promise to hear all prayers that proceed from the heart; and the prayer offered for one who loves us, and is dear to us, is sure to be heartfelt and fervent.

***

Hast thou no favors to ask of Me? Give Me, if thou wilt, a list of all thy desires, all the wants of thy soul. Tell Me, simply, of all thy pride, sensuality, self-love, sloth; and ask for My help in thy struggles to overcome them.

Poor child! be not abashed; many that had the same faults to contend against are now saints in heaven.

They cried to Me for help, and by degrees they conquered.

Do not hesitate to ask for temporal blessings,—health, intellect, success. I can bestow them, and never fail to do so, where they tend to make the soul more holy. What wouldst thou this day, My child? . . . If thou didst but know how I long to bless thee! . . .

❋

Hast thou no interests which occupy thy mind?

Tell Me of them all. . . . Of thy vocation. What dost thou think? What dost thou desire? Wouldst thou give pleasure to thy mother, thy family, those in authority over thee? what wouldst thou do for them?

And for Me hast thou no ardor?
Dost thou not desire to do some good
to the souls of those thou lovest, but
who are forgetful of Me?

Tell Me of one in whom thou hast
interest; the motive that actuates; the
means thou wouldst employ.

Lay before Me thy failures, and *I*
will teach thee the cause.

Whom wouldst thou have to help
thee? The hearts of all are in My
keeping, and *I* lead them gently where-
soever *I* will. Rest assured, all who
are needful to thee, *I* will place around
thee.

*Oh! My child, tell Me of all thy
weariness:* who has grieved thee?
treated thee with contempt? wounded
thy self-love?

Tell Me all, and thou wilt end by
saying, all is forgiven, all forgotten . . . and *I,* surely *I* will bless
thee! . . .

Art thou fearful of the future? Is

there in thy heart that vague dread that thou canst not define, but which never-theless torments thee?

Trust in My Providence. . . . *I* am present with thee, *I* know all, and *I* will never leave thee nor forsake thee.

Are there around thee those seem-ingly less devout than formerly, whose coldness or indifference have es-tranged thee from them without real cause? . . .

Pray for them. *I* can draw them back to thee if they are necessary to the sanctification of thy soul.

What are the joys of which thou hast to tell Me?

Let Me share thy pleasures; tell Me of all that has occurred since yester-day to comfort thee, please thee, to give thee joy!

That fear suddenly dispelled, that unexpected success, that token of af-

fection, the trial that proved thee
stronger than thou thoughtest. . . .

My child, *I* sent it all; why not show
some gratitude, and simply thank thy
LORD?

Gratitude draws down a blessing,
and the Great Benefactor likes His
children to remind Him of His Goodness.

*Hast thou no promises to make to
Me? I* can read thy heart; thou knowest it; thou mayst deceive man, but
thou canst never deceive GOD. Be sincere.

*Art thou resolved to avoid all occa-
sions of sin?* To renounce that which
tempts thee; never again to open the
book that excites thine imagination?
Not to bestow thine affection on one
who is not devout, and whose presence
steals the peace from thy soul?

Wilt thou go now and be loving and
forbearing towards one who has vexed
thee? . . .

Good, My child! . . . Go, then, return to thy daily toil; be silent, humble, resigned, charitable; then return to Me with a heart yet more loving and devoted, and *I* shall have for thee fresh blessings.

XXIII.

"THERE will soon be none left," said S. Francis de Sales, "who will love poor sinners but GOD and myself."

Oh! why do we fail in love towards those poor sinful ones! Are they not very much to be pitied?

When they are prosperous, pray for them; but when misfortune comes (and trouble weighs heavily upon the wicked), death depriving them of the only beings they did not hate, afflicting them with a loathsome disease, delivering them up to scorn and misery—oh! then, when all this comes upon them, love them freely. It is by affection alone that we can reach the worst characters, and the souls that are steeped in sin.

How many have died impenitent, who, if only some one had cared for them and shown them love, might have become at last saints in heaven! Oh! the sins that are committed, oh! the souls we suffer to wander from GOD, and all because we are so wanting in love towards them.

XXIV.

LET us always be on our guard against *Prejudice*.

Some women have a way (of which they themselves are unconscious) of turning the cold shoulder to some one member of their family.

For what reason? They cannot say, simply because the cause is never very clearly defined and in this lies all the mischief.

Perhaps an air of indifference they may have fancied, and which arose merely from fatigue, or trouble that could not be confided to them.

A word misinterpreted, because heard at a time when they felt discontented, and their morbid imagination made everything appear in a false light.

Some scandal to which they ought never to have listened, or, at least, should have endeavored to fathom, going direct to the person concerned and seeking an explanation.

And behold the result: they in their turn become cold, reserved, and suspicious, misinterpreting the slightest gesture . . . in a few days arises a coldness, from the feeling they are no longer beloved; then follow contempt and mistrust, finally, a hatred that gnaws and rends the very heart.

It all springs up imperceptibly, till

at last the family life is one of bitterness and misery.

They console, or better still, excuse themselves, with the thought of their suffering, never considering how much pain they give to others, nor where the fault lies.

XXV.

LET it rest! Ah! how many hearts on the brink of anxiety and disquietude by this simple sentence have been made calm and happy!

Some proceeding has wounded us by its want of tact; *let it rest;* no one will think of it again.

A harsh or unjust sentence irritates us; *let it rest;* whoever may have given vent to it will be pleased to see it is forgotten.

A painful scandal is about to estrange us from an old friend; *let it rest,* and thus preserve our charity and peace of mind.

A suspicious look is on the point of cooling our affection; *let it rest,* and our look of trust will restore confidence. . . .

Fancy! we who are so careful to remove the briers from our pathway for fear they should wound, yet take pleasure in collecting and piercing our hearts with the thorns that meet us in our daily intercourse with one another. How childish and unreasonable we are!

XXVI.

OF all the means placed by Providence within our reach, whereby we may lead souls to Him, there is one more blessed than all others,—intercessory prayer.

*

How often, in the presence of one deeply loved, but, alas! estranged from GOD, the heart of mother or wife

has felt a sudden impulse to say an
earnest word, propose an act of devotion, to paint in glowing colors the
blessings of faith and the happiness of
virtue . . . and she has stopped, de-
terred by an irresistible fear of how
the words may be received; and she
says to herself, poor woman, "To-morrow I shall be braver."

❋

Poor mother! poor wife! go and tell
to your Heavenly FATHER all you
would, but *dare* not, say to the loved
one who gives you so much pain.

Lay that sin-sick soul before the
LORD, as long ago they laid the para-
lytic man who could not, or perhaps
would not, be led to Him.

Plead for him with the long-suffering SAVIOUR, as you would plead with
an earthly master, upon whom depended all his future welfare, and say

to Him simply, "LORD, have patience with him yet a little longer."

Tell GOD of all your anxiety, your discouragements, the means employed for success.

Ask Him to teach you what to say and how to act. One sentence learned of GOD in prayer will do more for the conversion of a soul than all our poor human endeavors. *That* sentence will escape our lips involuntarily. We may not remember that we have said it, but it will sink deep into the heart, making a lasting impression, and silently fulfilling its mission.

❋

You are, perhaps, surprised, after many years, to see such poor results. Ah! how little can you judge! . . .

Do you know what you have gained? In the first place, time—often a physical impossibility to sin, which you may attribute to chance, but which was, in reality, the work of Providence; and is it nothing, one sin the less, in the life of an immortal soul? . . . Then a vague uneasiness which will soon allow of no rest, a confidence which may enable you to sympathize, more liberty left you for the exercise of religious acts; you no longer see the contemptuous smile at your acts of devotion. Is all this *nothing?*

Ah! if, while on your knees praying for the one you would have reconciled to GOD, you could but see what is passing in his soul,—the wrestlings, the remorse he strives vainly to stifle; if you could see the work of the Holy Spirit in the heart, gently but firmly triumphing over the will, how earnestly, how incessantly, would you continue to pray!

Only have patience to wait—perseverance not to grow weary.

It is the want of patience that often

makes us exacting towards those we
desire to help.

More haste, less speed, is an old
saying; the more we are exacting, the
less likely are we to succeed.

Men like to act freely, and to have
the credit of their actions.

It is because we have not learned to
persevere that the work seems never
to progress.

Courage, then! the ground may
seem too dry for cultivation, but each
prayer will be as a drop of water; the
marble may be very hard, but each
prayer is like the hammer's stroke that
wears away its roughness.

XXVII.

THE sweet peace of GOD bears the
outward token of resignation.

When the Holy Spirit dwells within
us everything seems bright.

Everything may not be exactly as

we would wish it, but we accept all with a good grace. . . . For instance, some change in our household or mode of living upsets us. If GOD is with us, He will whisper, "Yield cheerfully thy will; in a little while all will be forgotten."

Some command or employment wounds our pride; if GOD is with us, He will say to us, "Be submissive, and *I* will come to thine aid."

We may dislike a certain neighborhood; the society there may be repulsive to us, and we are about to become morbid: GOD will tell us to continue gracious and smiling, for He will recompense the little annoyances we may experience. If you would discern in whom GOD's Spirit dwells, watch that person, and notice whether you ever hear him murmur.

XXVIII.

I Want to Be Holy

HEAVENLY FATHER, aid Thy child, who longs to become holy! But then, I must be patient under humiliation, let myself be forgotten, and be even pleased at feeling myself set aside.

Never mind! I am resolved; I wish to be holy!

But I must never excuse myself, never be impatient, never out of temper.

Never mind! I am resolved; I wish to be holy!

Then I must continually be doing violence to my feelings,—submitting my will always to that of my superiors, never contentious, never sulky, finishing every work begun, in spite of dislike or ennui.

Never mind! I am resolved; I wish to be holy!

But then, I must be always charitable towards all around me; loving them, helping them to the utmost of my power, although it may cause me trouble.

Never mind! I am resolved; I wish to be holy!

But I must constantly strive against the cowardice, sloth, and pride of my nature, renouncing the world, the vanity that pleases, the sensuality that rejoices me, the antipathy that makes me avoid those I do not like.

Never mind! I am resolved; I still wish to be holy!

Then, I shall have to experience long hours of weariness, sadness, and discontent. I shall often feel lonely and discouraged.

Never mind! I am resolved; I wish to be holy! for then I shall have Thee always with me, ever near me. LORD, help me, for I want to be holy!

※

How to Become Holy

Oh! it is quite easy, if I fulfil every duty to the best of my ability; and many who had no more to do than I have become saints.

One day is the same as another. Prayer, worldly business, calls to be devout, charitable, and faithful,—these are the duties that each hour brings in its turn; and if I am faithful in their fulfilment, God will be always ready to help me, and then what signifies a little ennui, pain, or misfortune?

✳

The Sanctification of Daily Duties

I will perform them as in God's sight, conscious that He is present, and smiling on my efforts.

I will perform each as if I had but

one to accomplish, striving to render it
as perfect as possible.

I will fulfil each duty as if upon that
one alone depended my salvation.

❋

Motives for Sanctifying My Actions

God expects me to honor Him by
that action.

God has attached a special blessing
to that action, and awaits its fulfilment
to bestow it.

God notes each action; and of them
all hereafter I must give an account.

God will see that I love Him, if I
strive to fulfil every duty, in spite of
weariness and trouble.

I honor God by this action; and I,
poor, weak, sinful child, am allowed to
glorify Him, in place of those who
blaspheme and rebel against the Divine
will.

XXIX.

THEY say there is nothing which communicates itself so quickly amongst the members of a family as an expression of coldness or discontent on the face of one of its members. It is like the frost that chills us. This is not altogether true; there is something which is communicated with equal rapidity and greater force—I mean the smiling face, the beaming countenance, the happy heart.

XXX.

LITTLE WORRIES

THERE is not a day in our lives that we are not distressed by some one of those numberless little worries that meet us at every step, and which are inevitable.

The wound made may not be deep; but the constant pricks, each day re-

newed, imbitter the character, destroy
peace, create anxiety, and make the
family life, that otherwise would be so
sweet and peaceful, almost unendur-
able.

Life is full of these little miseries.
Each hour brings with it its own
trouble.

Here are, some of the little worries:
An impatient word escapes our lips
in the presence of some one in whose
estimation we would stand well.

A servant does his work badly,
fidgets us by his slowness, irritates us
by his thoughtlessness, and his awk-
ward blunders make us blush.

A giddy child in its clumsiness
breaks something of value, or that we
treasure on account of its associations;
we are charged with a message of importance, and our forgetfulness makes
us appear uncourteous, perhaps ungrateful; some one we live with is constantly finding fault, nothing pleases

them. If, when night comes, we find we have not experienced these little worries, then we ought to be grateful to GOD. Each of these, and many more, are liable to befall us every day of our life.

※

HOW TO BEAR LITTLE WORRIES

In the first place, expect them. Make them the subject of our morning prayers, and say to ourselves, Here is my daily cross, do I accept willingly? Surely! for it is GOD Who sends it. After all . . . these little troubles, looked at calmly, what are they? Ah, if there were never any worse!

Secondly, we must be prepared for them. You know, if you wish to break the force of a blow falling on you, you naturally bend the body; so let us act with regard to our souls.

Accustom yourself, wrote a pious

author, to stoop with sweet condescension, not only to exigencies (that is your duty), but to the simple wishes of those who surround you—the accidents which may intervene; you will find yourself seldom, if ever, crushed.

To *bend* is better than to *bear;* to bear is often a little hard; to bend implies a certain external sweetness that yields all constraint, sacrificing the wishes, even in holy things, when they tend to cause disagreements in the family circle.

Submission often implies an entire resignation to all that GOD permits. The soul that endures feels the weight of its trouble. The soul that yields scarcely perceives it.

Blessed are those docile ones; they are those whom GOD selects to work for Him.

XXXI.

To Obtain Peace

APPROACH the Blessed Sacrament, O restless soul, in search of peace, and, humbly kneeling there, pour forth bravely, slowly, and with earnest desire, the following prayer:—

O JESUS, gentle and humble of heart, hear me!

From the desire of being esteemed,
From the desire of being loved,
From the desire to be sought,

           Deliver me, JESUS.

From the desire to be mourned,
From the desire of praise,
From the desire of preference,
From the desire of influence,
From the desire of approval,
From the desire of authority,
From the fear of humiliation,
From the fear of being despised,
From the fear of repulse,

From the fear of calumny,
From the fear of oblivion,
From the fear of ridicule,
From the fear of injury,
From the fear of suspicion,

> Deliver me, JESUS.

That others may be loved more than myself. JESUS grant this desire.

That others may be more highly esteemed.

That others may grow and increase in honor, and I decrease. JESUS, grant me to desire it.

That others may be employed, and I set aside. JESUS, grant me to desire this.

That others may attract the praise, and myself be forgotten.

That others may be preferred in all.

Grant me the utmost holiness of which I am capable, then let others be holier than myself. JESUS, grant me to desire it!

Oh, if GOD hearkens,—and hearken He surely will, if your prayer has been sincere,—what joy in your heart, what peace on your countenance, what sweetness will pervade your whole life!

More than half one's troubles arise from an exaggerated idea of one's own importance, and the efforts we make to increase our position in the world. Lacordaire says, that the sweetest thing on earth is to be forgotten by all, with the exception of those who love us. All else brings more trouble than joy; and as soon as we have completed our task here, and fulfilled our mission, the best thing for us to do is to disappear altogether.

❋

Let us each cultivate carefully and joyously the portion of soil Providence has committed to our care. Let us never be hindered or distracted by

ambitious thoughts, that we could do
better, or a false zeal tempting us to
forsake our daily task with the vain
desire to surpass our neighbors. . . .
Let this one thought occupy our minds.
To do *well* what is given us to do, for
this is all that GOD requires at our
hands. It may be summed up in four
words,—simply, zealously, cheerfully,
completely.

※

Then if we *are* slighted, misunderstood, maligned, or persecuted, what
does it matter? These injuries will
pass away; but the peace and love of
GOD will remain with us forever, the
reward of our faith and patience. The
love of GOD! Who can describe all the
joy, strength, and consolation it reveals?

Never has human love, in its bright-
est dreams, been able to form any idea
of all the sweetness the love of GOD

imparts to the soul, and which is brought still nearer to us in the Blessed Sacrament.

I can well understand the words of a loving soul: "With heaven so near, and daily communion with our GOD, how can we ever repine!"

XXXII.

AFTER HOLY COMMUNION

OUR FATHER WHICH ART IN HEAVEN

O JESUS! it is Thou Who biddest me say, FATHER! *My Father!* Oh how that Name rejoices my heart! *My Father!* I can no longer feel alone; and whatever may happen to me this day, I feel I am protected, comforted, beloved.

JESUS! let me dwell on the sweetness of those words: *My Father!* I need not lift my eyes to heaven, Thou art within me, and where Thou dwellest heaven must be.

Yes! heaven is within me! heaven with all its peace and love; and if I keep free from guile this day, my day will be one of heavenly joy, and in addition, the privilege of suffering for Thee.

HALLOWED BE THY NAME

To hallow Thy Name, O LORD, is to pronounce it with reverence and awe.

To-day I will pray more fervently, try to realize Thy Presence, Thy Goodness, Thy Love; and my heart shall be a sanctuary into which nothing shall penetrate that could be displeasing unto Thee.

To *hallow Thy Name* is to call upon it fervently, to have it constantly upon my lips; above all, before taking an important step, when there are difficulties to be overcome, I will softly whisper the Invocation, which is the secret of all holy living! "Jesus, meek and humble of heart, have pity upon me."

THY KINGDOM COME

O Jesus, Thy kingdom is within my heart, reign there in all Thy sovereignty and power, reign there absolutely!

My King! what dost Thou require of me to-day? Thy commandments, my rule of life, my daily duties,—these are Thy commands that I will promise to obey; more than that, I will regard all in authority over me as Thine Ambassadors, speaking to me in Thy Name. What matters the tone or the harshness of the order?

What does it signify if some unexpected command upsets all my previous plans? It is Thy Voice I hear, Thou Lord, Whom I will obey always, and in all things.

Thy kingdom is also in the hearts of

others; and there would I see Thee
reigning. Then to whom can I speak
of Thee this day? What counsels can
I give? What moments may I seize,
in which, without wounding the feelings, or parading my zeal, I may be
allowed to speak a few words of piety?
LORD, let me have the opportunity to
help another to love Thee!

THY WILL BE DONE IN EARTH, AS IT IS IN HEAVEN

Yes, yes! Thy Will be done! Thy
sweet all-perfect Will!

What wilt Thou send me to-day?

Humiliation? Provocation? Sufferings? A fresh rending of the heart?
A disappointment? Shall I see myself misjudged, falsely suspected, despised? I accept beforehand all that
Thou sendest me; and if through
weakness I weep, suffer it to be so; if
I murmur, check me; if I am vexed,
correct me; if hopeless, encourage me.

Yes, yes! Let Thy sweet and holy Will be done!

Even, O LORD, if to glorify Thee, I must be humiliated, suffering, useless, and forsaken, still, LORD, stay not Thine Hand, I am wholly Thine.

GIVE US THIS DAY OUR DAILY BREAD

How blessed, O LORD, to depend only upon Thee . . . behold me, Thy child, waiting with outstretched hand to receive Thy benefits.

Grant me my temporal blessings,— clothing, nourishment, shelter . . . but not too much of anything; and let me have the happiness of sharing my blessings with those poorer than my-self to-day. Grant me the blessing of intelligence, that I may read, or hear one of those golden counsels that ele-vate the soul, and lend wings to the thoughts.

Grant me the loving heart, O my

FATHER! that I may feel for a moment how I love Thee, and Thy love towards me; let me sacrifice myself for the welfare of another. Give me the Bread of Life, the Holy Eucharist! I have just received it, LORD! Grant me again ere long that great blessing.

And then, give all these blessings to those I love, and who love me!

FORGIVE US OUR TRESPASSES, AS WE FORGIVE THEM THAT TRESPASS AGAINST US

When I pronounce the word of pardon, what a weight seems lifted from my heart.

I will not only banish every feeling of hatred, I will efface every painful remembrance. O GOD, if Thou forgivest me, as I forgive others, what mercy for me!

Thou seest I bear no malice, that I forget all injuries. . . .

I have been offended by *words;* I forget them; by actions, I forget them; by omissions, thoughts, desires; they are all forgotten.

Ah! in all these ways I have offended Thee, and Thou wilt forget, even as I have forgotten.

I will be very merciful, so that Thou mayst have mercy upon me.

LEAD US NOT INTO TEMPTATION, BUT DELIVER US FROM EVIL

Now, as I leave Thine altar, I go to encounter temptation.

O SAVIOUR! help me, keep me, and warn me of my danger!

Let me shun all occasions of evil, and if by weakness or allurements I am led into paths of sin, if I fall, oh! rescue me speedily, that I may fall upon my knees, confessing my sin, and imploring pardon.

Sin! this is the evil from which I beseech Thee to deliver me; other

troubles that may happen, I accept;
they are sent to try me and to purify,
and come from Thee; but sin, I have
no pleasure in it! Oh! when in the
hour of temptation I fall away, LORD,
hearken to the cry that I now raise
to Thee in all sincerity; I *will* it not!
it is not wilful! I go from Thy Presence, but, JESUS, Thou art with me!
In work, in prayer, in suffering, let all
be done in Thee!

XXXIII.

"MOTHER," asked a child, "since
nothing is ever lost, where do
all our thoughts go?"

"To GOD," answered the mother
gravely, "who remembers them forever."

"Forever!" said the child. He bent
his head, and, drawing closer to his
mother, murmured, "I am frightened!"

Which of us have not felt the same?

XXXIV.

ONE more solemn thought: How old are you? Nineteen. Have you reckoned the number of minutes that have elapsed since your birth? The number is startling: nine millions, three hundred and thirty-three thousand, two hundred. . . . Each of those minutes has flown to GOD; GOD has examined them and weighed them, and for them you must give account.

Each minute bears its own impress (as a coin bears the impress of the Sovereign), and only those marked with the image of GOD will avail you for eternity.

Is not this thought one to make you tremble?

"I never could understand," writes Guérin, "the feeling of security some have that their works must find favor with GOD—as if our duties were confined to the narrow limits of this little world. To be a good son, statesman, or brother, is not all that is required of us; GOD demands far more than this from those for whom He has destined a crown of glory hereafter."

XXXV.

ONE great characteristic of holiness is never to be exacting, never to complain.

Each complaint drags us down a degree in our upward course.

By complaining, I do not mean the simple imparting of our troubles to others.

Complaint savors always of a little bad temper, and a slightly vindictive spirit

✻

The saints were never exacting.

Contented with their lot, they never desired anything that was withheld from them.

"I have asked," said a holy soul, "for something I thought needful; they have forgotten to answer me, or perhaps would not bestow it. Why need I be disquieted? If it were really necessary, GOD would quickly provide means to obtain it." How few could enter into this feeling; and yet it is but the echo of CHRIST'S own words, "Your FATHER in Heaven knoweth that ye have need of all these things."

XXXVI.

JOY in life is like oil in a lamp. When the oil gets low the wick is consumed, emitting a black vapor, and sending forth only a lurid glow, which does not give light.

A life without joy passes away unprofitably, shedding around it only gloom and sorrow.

If every morning in a simple prayer, —in those fifteen minutes' meditation (which only seem hard when we do not practise it),—we opened our hearts to God, as we open our windows to the sun and air, God would fill it with that calm, sweet joy which elevates the soul, prevents it feeling the weight of troubles, and makes it overflow with benevolence.

But joy does not mean levity, witty sayings, or repartee . . . it is habitual serenity.

Through a clear atmosphere we can always see the sky; it seems so light and full of elasticity.

A serene sky is always pure . . . clouds may pass across it, but they do not stain it.

So it is with the heart that early in the morning opens to receive God's Peace.

XXXVII.

"YOU are never out of temper," was once said to a woman well known to be much tried at home; "is it that you do not feel the injustice, the annoyances?"—"I feel them as much as you do," she replied; "but they do not hurt me."—"You have, then, some special balm?"—"Yes; for the vexations caused by people, I have *affection;* for those of circumstances, I have prayer; and over every wound that bleeds, I murmur the words, 'Thy Will be done.'"

XXXVIII.

MY DAILY CROSS

IF I have no cross to bear to-day, I shall not advance heavenwards.

A cross (that is, anything that disturbs our peace) is the spur which stimulates, and without which we should most likely remain stationary, blinded with empty vanities, and sinking deeper into sin.

A cross helps us onwards, in spite of our apathy and resistance.

To lie quietly on a bed of down may seem a very sweet existence, but pleasant ease and rest are not the lot of a Christian; if he would mount higher and higher, it must be by a rough road.

Alas, for those who have no daily cross!

Alas, for those who repine and fret against it!

※

WHAT WILL BE MY CROSS TO-DAY?

Perhaps that person with whom Providence has placed me, and whom I dislike, whose look of disdain humiliates me, whose slowness worries me, who makes me jealous by being more beloved, more successful, than myself, whose chatter and light-heartedness, even her very attentions to myself, annoy me.

Or it may be that person that I think has quarrelled with me, and my

imagination makes me fancy myself
watched, criticised, turned into ridicule.

She is always with me; all my efforts to separate are frustrated; by
some mysterious power she is always
present, always near.

✤

This is my heaviest cross; the rest
are light in comparison.

Circumstances change, temptations
diminish, troubles lessen; but those
people who trouble or offend us are
an ever-present source of irritation.

How to Bear This Daily Cross

Never manifest, in any way, the
ennui, the dislike, the involuntary
shudder, that her presence produces;
force myself to render her some little
service—never mind if she never
knows it; it is between God and myself. Try to say a little good of her

every day, of her talents, her character,
her tact, for there is all that to be
found in her. Pray earnestly for her,
even asking GOD to help me to love
her, and to spare her to me.

Dear companion! blessed messenger
of GOD's mercy! you are, without
knowing it, the means for my sanctification, and I will not be ungrateful.

Yes! though the exterior be rude
and repellent, yet to you I owe it that
I am kept from greater sin; you,
against whom my whole nature re-
bels . . . how I ought to love you!

XXXIX.

WHO is anxious for a beloved one's
eternal welfare?

We interest ourselves for their success, their prosperity; we ask GOD to
keep them from harm and misfortune;
we try to start them well in the world,
to make them of reputation, to procure
them pleasure.

To spare them trouble, we sacrifice our own ease and enjoyment. . . .

Oh, that is all very beautiful, very right; but what should we do for the soul?

Do we pray to GOD that this soul may become humble, pure, devoted?

Do we take as much pains to procure him the little devotional book that will really help him, as we should to obtain a transient pleasure?

Do we help him, unseen, towards that act of charity, humiliation, or self renunciation? Have we courage not to spare the soul the trial that we know will purify?

Does it seem too hard for you?

Ah! then you do not know what real love is. Does not GOD love us? Yet GOD lets us suffer; even sends the suffering.

Love is given us to help us onwards, nearer to GOD. The most blessed is that which draws us nearest to Him;

and in proportion as it leads to GOD we realize its blessedness.

The essence of true love is not its *tenderness,* but its strength, power of endurance, its purity, its self-renunciation.

The mistake we make is when we seek to be beloved, instead of loving. What makes us cowardly is the fear of losing that love.

Never forget this: A selfish heart desires love for itself; a Christian heart delights to love—without return.

XL.

TO learn never to waste our time is perhaps one of the most difficult virtues to acquire.

A well-spent day is a source of pleasure. To be constantly employed, and never asking, "What shall I do?" is the secret of much goodness and happiness.

Begin, then, with promptitude, act decisively, persevere; if interrupted, be amiable, and return to the work unruffled, finish it carefully—these will be the signs of a virtuous soul.

XLI.

ARE you full of peace? *Pray!* Prayer will preserve it to you.

Are you tempted? *Pray!* Prayer will sustain you.

Have you fallen? *Pray!* Prayer will raise you.

Are you discouraged? *Pray!* Prayer will reassure and comfort you.

XLII.

THE young are seldom forbearing, because they so little understand the frailties of poor human nature.

Oh! if you could only witness the terrible struggles passing in the heart of that friend whose vivacity annoys you, whose fickleness provokes you, whose faults sometimes even make you blush. . . .

Oh! if you saw the tears that are shed in secret, the vexation felt against self (perhaps on your account), you would indeed pity them. Love them! make allowances for them! never let them feel that you know their failings.

To make any one believe himself good, is to help him almost in spite of self to become so.

❋

Forbearance is even *more* than forgiveness; it is excusing, putting always the best construction upon everything; above all, never showing that some proceeding has wounded us; speaking of any one who has vexed us thus: "She did not think, else she would have acted differently; she never meant to pain me, she loves me too much; she was perhaps unable to do otherwise, and yet suffers at the thought of having displeased me."

For a wounded heart no balm is so efficacious as forbearance.

To forbear is to forget every night the little vexations of the past day; to say every morning: "To-day I shall be braver and calmer than yesterday." Forbearance even sometimes leads us to detect in ourselves a little want of good nature, condescension, and charity.

To forbear is not only freely to forgive, but to meet half-way, with extended hand, those who timidly ask for pardon.

XLIII.

MY friend, do you know why the work you accomplish fails either to give pleasure to yourself or others?

It is because it is not cheerfully done, and therefore appears discolored.

A joyous heart amid our work imparts to duty a brilliancy that charms the eyes of others, while it prevents those feeling wounded who cannot perform it equally well.

Joy, with us, is like a lever, by which we lift the weights that without its help would crush us.

A workman once said: "If I were to leave off singing, I should be quite unequal to my business."

Then sing always; let your heart sing as in its earliest years.

The refrain of the heart, which perhaps never passes the lips, but which echoes in heaven, is this sentence:—

"I love and I am beloved!"

XLIV.

WHAT regret we sometimes feel, after the death or departure of friends, at never having shown them the respect, the gratitude, we felt towards them, and how from the depths of our heart we are filled with tenderness and affection for them!

It may have been that at times we could not speak, because we thought too much of *how* to say it.

Another time we lost the opportunity, because we were always shirking it. Deep devotion is sometimes a little erratic; always afraid of doing too little, doing it badly or inopportunely. Oftener still the tokens of affection are checked, because we think we could show it in some better way; we put off till brighter days the dreams we cherished, the sweet yearning to open the heart to the loved ones, and let them see for once what a large place they fill there.

Alas! the days fly past, suddenly comes death, or, sadder still, separation without hope of return, leaving the bitter thought: "Others will show them better than I have done, how dear, how valued, they are." Ah! when we can be loving *to-day,* never let us say, "I will love to-morrow;" when we have the opportunity of being grateful, never put off, for *one* hour, the proof of our gratitude!

❊

CONCLUSION

LACORDAIRE, in preparing for a retreat in the country, said he only required for his realization of a dream of happiness and solitude, three things,—(1) GOD; (2) a friend; (3) books.

God!—We never fail to find Him when we are pure, holy, and fulfilling hourly our duty.

A Friend!—Responds always to the heart's call, if only that heart be loving and devoted.

Books!—Oh! if only this little book of *Gold Dust* might be allowed to form one of the numbers of those that are carried away, far from the world's turmoil, and read in order to gain a little help and peace!

It will take up *so* little room!

GOLD DUST

I.

THE FRIENDLY WHISPER

UNDER this title we commence a
series of short counsels for each
day of the week, which will be as a
friendly whisper, the voice of a Guardian Angel, inspiring, as occasion presents itself, some good action, some
self-denial, some little sacrifice.

We recommend that it should be
placed on the writing-table, in the book
we most frequently turn to, or wherever it is most likely to meet the eye.
What is so often the one thing want-

ing to some devout person devoted to
doing good? Simply to be *reminded*.

MONDAY

CHARITY

BE good-natured, benevolent, keep
up a cheerful expression of countenance, even when alone.

That clumsiness, those brusque, rude
manners, let them pass without notice.

When wishes contrary to your own
prevail, yield without ill-humor, or
even showing your effort; you will
give pleasure, and thus be pleased
yourself.

Try to please, to console, to amuse,
to bestow, to thank, to help. That is
all in itself so good!

Try to do some good to the souls
of others! An earnest word, some encouragement, a prayer softly breathed.

Overcome your dislike and aversion
to certain persons; do not shun them,

on the contrary go and meet them.
GOD goes before you.

Be courteous even to the trouble-
some individual who is always in your
way. GOD sends him to you.

Forgive at once. Do you believe
harm was intended? If so, is it not
the greater merit?

Do not refuse your alms, only let
your motives be pure; and in giving,
give as to GOD.

Do not judge the guilty harshly;
pity, and pray for them.

Why imagine evil intentions against
yourself? cannot you see how the
thought troubles and disquiets you?

Check the ironical smile hovering
about your lips; you will grieve the
object of it. Why cause any one pain?

Lend yourself to all. GOD will not
suffer you to be taken advantage of
if you are prompted by the spirit of
Charity.

TUESDAY

THE DIVINE PRESENCE

NEVER separate yourself from GOD. How sweet it is to live always near those who love us!

You cannot see GOD, but He is there; just as if some friend were separated from you by a curtain, which does not prevent his seeing you, and which at any moment may unfold and disclose him to your view.

When the soul is unstained by sin, and if we remain still and recollected, we can perceive GOD's presence in the heart, just as we see daylight penetrating a room. We may not be always conscious of this Presence, but imperceptibly it influences all our actions. Oh! however heavy may be the burden you have to bear, does it not at once become light beneath the gaze of that FATHER's eye?

The thought of GOD is never wearisome; why not always cherish it? Go on, without trembling, beneath the Eye of GOD; never fear to smile, love, hope, and enjoy all that makes life sweet.

GOD rejoices in our pleasures as a mother in the joys of her child.

What is contrary to GOD'S Will, grieves Him, and does you harm, that alone you need fear,—the thought that will stain your soul; the wish that troubles your heart; that unwholesome action, that will weaken your intellect, and destroy your peace.

Never long for what GOD sees fit to deny.

GOD, beside you, will repair your blunders, provide means whereby you may atone for that sinful action by one more virtuous, wipe away the tears caused by some unmerited reproof or unkind word.

You have only to close your eyes for a moment, examine yourself, and softly murmur, "LORD, help me!"

Can you not hear God's Voice speaking to you? What! when He says: *Bear this, I am here to aid thee;* you will refuse?

He says: *Continue another half-hour the work that wearies thee;* and you would stop?

He says: *Do not that;* and you do it?

He says: *Let us tread together the path of obedience;* and you answer: No?

WEDNESDAY

SELF-RENUNCIATION

DO not be afraid of that word *Renunciation.* To you, perhaps, it only means, weariness, restraint, ennui. But it means also, love, perfection, sanctification.

✳

Who cannot renounce, cannot love. Who cannot renounce, cannot become perfect.

Who cannot renounce, cannot be made holy.

❋

Self-renunciation, means devotion to our duty, going on with it in spite of difficulties, disgust, ennui, want of success.

Self-renunciation is self-sacrifice, under whatever form it presents itself, —*prayer, labor, love* . . . all that would be an obstacle, not merely to its accomplishment, but its perfection.

Self-renunciation is to root out all that encumbers the heart, all that impedes the free action of the Holy Spirit within—longings after an imaginary perfection or well-being, unreal sentiments that trouble us in prayer, in work, in slumber, that fascinate us, but the result of which is to destroy all real application.

Self-renunciation is to resist all the allurements of the senses, that would only give pleasure to self, and satisfy the conscience, by whispering, *"It is no sin."* *Self-renunciation,* in short, is destroying, even at the risk of much heart-rending, all in our heart, mind, imagination, that could be displeasing to GOD.

Renunciation is not one single action, that when once accomplished we experience relief; it means a constant *sacrifice, restraint, resisting, rending,* each hour, each moment, during our whole life.

But is not this a worry, a continual torment? No; not if the moving spring be love or godly fear . . .

Do you consider it a trouble when you make yourself less comfortable to make room for a friend who visits you?

Well! there are times when GOD would make you sensible of His Presence. He is with you, and to retain

Him close, Who is all Purity, will you not be more modest in your behavior?

If you would receive Him into your heart at Holy Communion, will you not make room for Him, by rooting out that affection He has pointed out to you as dangerous, that interest, that desire, that worldly, sensual attachment?

Oh! if you only *really* loved.

Would you call it *torture* or *constraint,* the energy with which you shatter some poisoned cup you were almost enticed to drink?

Well! when encountering the attractive enjoyment, the material delight, which might lead you astray, or the siren voice which would allure you from your duty for a moment— then when conscience whispers, *"Beware,"* . . . would you be cowardly?

Alas, it is slowly and surely that the stream carries on to destruction the blossom that has fallen into its current.

It is little by little that pleasure leads on to sin the heart that lets itself be lulled by its charms.

THURSDAY

SUBMISSION

AS soon as you awake in the morning, try to realize GOD stretching forth His Hand towards you, and saying, *Dost thou really desire that I should watch over thee this day?* and you lift up your hands towards this kind FATHER, and say to Him, "Yes, yes, lead me, guide me, love me; I will be very submissive!"

Beneath GOD's protecting Hand, is it possible that you can be sorrowful, fearful, unhappy?

No; GOD will allow no suffering, no trial, above what you are able to bear.

Then pass through the day, quietly and calmly, even as when a little child you had your mother always beside you.

You need only be careful about *one* thing, *never to displease God,* and you will see how lovingly GOD will direct all that concerns you—material interests, sympathies, worldly cares; you will be astonished at the sudden enlightenment that will come to you, and the wondrous peace that will result from your labor and your toil.

Then, welcome trial, sickness, ennui, privations, injustice . . . all of it can only come directed by GOD's Hand, and will wound the soul only in order to cleanse some spot within.

Would your mother have given you a bitter dose merely for the sake of causing you suffering?

If your duty is hard, owing either to its difficulty or the distaste you feel towards it, lift your heart to GOD and say, *"Lord, help me,"* . . . then go on with it, even though you seem to do it imperfectly.

Should one of those moments of

vague misgivings, that leave the soul as it were in utter darkness, come to overwhelm you, call upon GOD, as a child in terror cries out to its mother.

If you have sinned, oh! even then be not afraid of the merciful GOD, but with eyes full of tears, say to Him, "Pardon me" . . . and add softly, "chastise me soon, O LORD!"

Yes, yes, dear one, be always at peace, going on quietly with your daily duties . . . more than that, be always joyous.

And why not?

You who have no longer a mother to love you, and yet crave for love, GOD will be as a mother. You who have no brother to help you, and have so much need of support, GOD will be your brother. You who have no friends to comfort you, and stand so much in need of consolation, GOD will be your friend.

Preserve always the *childlike sim-*

plicity which goes direct to GOD, and
speak to Him as you would speak to
your mother.

Keep that open *confidence* that tells
Him your projects, troubles, joys, as
you tell them to a brother.

Cherish those *loving words* that
speak of all the happiness you feel,
living in dependence upon Him, and
trusting in His Love, just as you
would tell it to the friend of your
childhood.

Keep the *generous heart of childhood* which gives all you have to GOD.
Let Him freely take whatever He
pleases, all within and around you.
Will only what He wills, desiring only
what is in accordance with His Will,
and finding nothing impossible that He
commands.

Do you not feel something soothing
and consoling in these thoughts? The
longer you live, the better you will understand that true happiness is only to

be found in a life devoted to GOD, and given up entirely to His Guidance.

No! no! none can harm you, unless it be GOD's Will, and if He allows it; be patient and humble, weep if your heart is sore, but love always, and wait . . . the trial will pass away, but GOD will remain yours forever.

FRIDAY

PRAYER

OH, if you only knew what it is to pray! oh, if GOD would only give you the grace to love prayer! What peace to your soul, what love in your heart!

What joy would shine in your countenance, even though the tears streamed from your eyes!

Prayer, as the first cry escapes the lips, indicates to GOD that some one would speak to Him, and GOD, so good and gracious, is ever ready to listen (with all reverence we say it), with the prompt attention of a faithful servant. He manifests Himself to the soul with ineffable love, and says to it, "Behold Me, thou hast called Me, what dost thou desire of Me?"

To pray is to remain, so long as our prayer lasts, in the Presence of GOD, with the certainty that we can never weary Him, no matter what may be the subject of our prayer, or at those times when we are speechless, and as in the case of the good peasant quoted by the Curé d'Ars, we are content to place ourselves before GOD, with only the recollection of His Presence.

To pray is to act towards GOD as the child does to its mother, the poor man towards the rich, eager to do him good, the friend towards his friend, who longs to show him affection.

Prayer is the key to all celestial treasures; by it we penetrate into the midst of all the joy, strength, mercy, and goodness Divine, . . . we receive our well-being from all around us, as the sponge plunged into the ocean imbibes without an effort the water that surrounds it . . . this joy, strength, mercy, and goodness become our own.

Oh, yes! if you knew how to pray, and loved prayer, how good, useful, fruitful, and meritorious would be your life!

Nothing so elevates the soul as prayer.

GOD, so condescending to the soul, raises it with Him to the regions of light and love, and then, the prayer finished, the soul returns to its daily duties with a more enlightened mind, a more earnest will. It is filled with radiance divine, and sheds of its abundance upon all who approach.

If you would succeed in your study, with the success that sanctifies, *pray* before commencing.

If you would succeed in your intercourse with others, pray before becoming intimate.

Nothing so smooths and sweetens life as *Prayer*.

There is the *solitary* prayer, when the soul isolated from all creatures is alone with GOD and feels thus towards Him: "GOD and I;" *God* to love; *I* to adore, praise, glorify, thank.

God to bestow, *I* humbly to receive, to renounce, ask, hope, submit! . . .

Ah! who can tell all that passes between the soul and its GOD?

There is the *united* prayer of two friends, bound together by a holy friendship, their desires and thoughts are one, and as one they present themselves before GOD, crying, "Have mercy upon me!"

There is the prayer of two hearts separated by distance, made at the same hour in the same words. Soothing prayer, that each day reunites those two sad hearts torn by the agony of parting, and who in GOD's Presence, strengthened with the same HOLY SPIRIT, recover courage to tread the road to heaven, each in its appointed sphere.

Then there is Public Prayer, that which has the special proimse of GOD's Presence; prayer so comforting to the feeble, guilty soul, who can cry in very truth, "My prayer ascends to GOD, supported by the prayers of others."

Oh! if you knew how to pray, and loved prayer, how happy and faithful would be your life!

SATURDAY

EARNESTNESS

YOU love GOD, do you not, dear one, whom GOD surrounds with so much affection?

Yes, yes! I love Him!

And how do you prove to Him your love?

I keep myself pure and innocent, so that His Eye falling upon me may never see anything that displeases Him. I keep myself calm and quiet, and force myself to smile that He may see I am contented.

That is right, but that is not enough.

I think often of how much I owe Him, and apply myself diligently to the work He has given me to do; I bear patiently with those I dislike, with troubles that irritate me; when I am weak I call upon Him, when timid I draw near to Him, when sinful I implore pardon, and strive to do my duty more faithfully.

That is right, but that is not enough.

I lend myself to the importunities of others. I am as a slave to those who need me, and take care never to judge any one harshly.

That is right, but still it is not enough.

Ah! then what more can I do, good angel, thus addressing me, what can I do to show my love to GOD?

Devote thyself to doing good to the souls of others.

Oh, if you knew how it pleases GOD to see you laboring for them! It is like the joy of a mother, every time she sees some one benefiting her child.

How thankful she is to those who nursed it in sickness, spared it pain, showed it some token of affection, a counsel, a warning, that gave it pleasure, by a kind word, a plaything, a smile!

All this you may do in that circle, more or less extended, in which you live.

Leave to GOD's minister, if you will, the work of converting souls, and limit your efforts to doing good by bringing yourself into communion with them.

To do so, means sweetly, uncon-

sciously, softly, spea to them of GOD,
carry them to GOD, lead them to GOD.

This may be done by gently, tenderly—by inference as it were—speaking to them of GOD, thus leading them
towards Him, bringing them into contact with Him.

Hearts are drawn together by talk-
ing of their kindred pursuits, souls by
speaking of heavenly things.

It is not necessary for this purpose
to pronounce the name of GOD; it will
suffice that the words shall lift the soul
beyond this material world and its
sensual enjoyments, and raise them
upwards to that supernatural atmosphere necessary to the real life.

Speak of the happiness of devotion,
the charm of purity, the blessing of the
few minutes' meditation at the feet of
JESUS, the peace procured by entire
resignation to Providence, and the
sweetness of a life spent beneath GOD's
Fatherly Eye, the comfort the thought

of heaven brings in the midst of trouble, the hope of the meeting again above, the certainty of eternal happiness. This is doing good to others, drawing them nearer to GOD, and teaching them more and more of holiness.

Limit your efforts to this; later on I will tell you what more you may do.

SUNDAY

SYMPATHY

WELCOME with joy each week the day that GOD has called His day.

To each day of the week GOD has given its special mission, its share of pleasure and of pain, necessary to purify and fortify and prepare us for eternity.

But *Sunday* is a day of *Love*.

On Saturday we lay aside our garments faded and stained by toil, and

on Sunday we array ourselves in garments, not only fresher, but more
choice and graceful.

Why not prepare the heart, even as
we do the body?

During the week has not the heart
been wearied with petty strife and
discontent, interests marred, bitter
words?

Then, why not shake off all this,
that only chills affection? On the
Saturday let us forgive freely, press
the hand warmly, embrace each other;
and then peace being restored within,
we await the morrow's awakening.

Sunday is GOD'S day of truce for
all. That day, laying aside all revenge
and ill-feeling, we must be filled with
forbearance, indulgence, and amiability.

Oh! how good for us to feel *obliged*
to be reconciled, and each Sunday re-
news the obligation.

Let us leave no time for coldness

and indifference to grow upon us . . .
it only engenders hatred, and that once
established in the heart, oh! how hard
is it to cast out again!

It is like a hideous cancer whose
ravages no remedies can stay.

It is as the venomous plant that the
gardener can never entirely eradicate.
Only by a miracle can hatred be destroyed. At once then let us place a
barrier in our hearts against the approach of coolness or indifference, and
each Saturday night the head of the
family shall thus address us: "Children, to-night we forgive, to-night we
forget, and to-morrow begin life
afresh in love, one towards another."

II.

WHEN I have sinned, wrote a
pious soul, I feel chastisement
will fall upon me, and as if I could
hide myself from GOD'S Eye. I *shrink*
into myself, and then I pray, I pray,

and the chastisement not being sent, I again expand.

Chastisement is like a stone threatening to crush me; *Prayer* is the hand that withholds it while I make atonement.

Oh! how can those live peacefully who never pray?

III.

OUR DEAD

THEY are not all there—our dead —buried in the churchyard, beneath the grave, o'ershadowed by a cross, and round which the roses bloom.

There are others which nothing can recall; they are things which belong to the *heart* alone, and there alas! have found a tomb.

Peace surrounds me to-day; and here in my lone chamber I will invoke them, my much-loved dead. Come!

✳

The first that present themselves are *the sweet years of childhood,* so fresh, so guileless, so happy.

They were made up of loving caresses, bountiful rewards, and fearless confidence: the words, *pain, danger, care,* were unknown; they brought me simple pleasures, happy days without a thought for the morrow, and only required from me a little obedience.

Alas! they are dead . . . and what numberless things have they carried with them! What a void they have left!

Candor, lightheartedness, simplicity, no longer find a place within!

Family ties, so true, so wide, so light, have all vanished!

The homely hearth, the simple reward earned by the day's industry, maternal chidings, forgiveness so ingenuously sought, so freely given, promises of amendment, so sincere.

so joyously received. . . . Is this all
gone forever? can I never recall them?

The vision that follows is that of my
early piety, simple and full of faith,
which was as some good angel o'er-
shadowing me with its snowy wings,
and showing me GOD everywhere, in
all, and with all.

The good GOD, Who each day provides my daily bread!

The GOD, Who spared my mother
in sickness, and relieved her when she
suffered—GOD, Who shielded me from
harm when I did right!

The GOD, Who sees all, knows all,
and is Omnipotent, Whom I loved
with all my heart.

Alas! faithful, simple piety, thou art
dead; in innocence alone couldst thou
live!

Next comes *the love of my earliest
years.* Love in childhood, love in
youth, so full of true, simple joy, that
initiated me in the sweet pleasure of

devotion, that taught me self-denial in order to give pleasure, that destroyed all egotism, by showing me the happiness of living for others.

Love of my childhood, love of my youth, so pure, so holy, on which I always reckoned when they spoke to me of trouble, loneliness, depression . . . thou also art dead.

An involuntary coolness, an unfounded suspicion never cleared, an ill-natured story . . . all these have destroyed that child of Heaven. I knew it was tender, and I cherished it, but I could not believe it to be so frail.

I could make a long list of all the dead enshrined in my heart! Oh, you who are still young, upon whom GOD has lavished all the gifts that are lost to me,—candor, simplicity, innocence, love, devotion . . . guard, oh, guard these treasures, and that they may never die, place them beneath the shelter of *Prayer*.

IV.

THE SPIRITUAL LIFE

WHAT a sweet life is that! The maintaining, strengthening it, has a softening influence; and it is a labor that never wearies, never deceives, but gives each day fresh cause for joy.

In the language of devotion, it is called the *interior life;* and it is our purpose to point out minutely its nature, excellence, means, and hindrances.

Let no one think the interior life is incompatible with the life domestic and social, which is often so engrossing; just as the action of the heart maintained by the constant flow of blood in no way affects the outward movements, so is it with the life of the soul, which consists chiefly in the action of GOD's HOLY SPIRIT within, that never hinders our social duties, but on

the contrary is a help towards fulfilling them more calmly, more perfectly.

❋

Nature of the Interior Life

The interior life is an abiding sense
of GOD's Presence, a constant union
with Him.

We learn to look upon the heart as
the temple where GOD dwells, sometimes glorious as above, sometimes hid-·
den as in the Holy Eucharist; and we
act, think, speak, and fulfil all our
duties, as in His Presence.

Its aim is to shun sin, and cultivate
a detachment from all earthly things
by a spirit of poverty; sensual pleasures by purity and mortification; pride
by humility; dissipation by recollection.

As a rule, people are prejudiced
against an interior life. Some are
afraid of it, and look upon it as a life
of bondage, sacrifice, and restraint;

others despise it, as nothing but a
multiplicity of trifling rules, tending
only to narrow-mindedness and use-
lessness, and fit only for weak minds.
In consequence they are on their
guard against it, and avoid the books
that treat of it.

They would serve GOD no doubt,
but they will not subject themselves to
the entire guidance of His Spirit; in
short, it is far easier to bring a soul
from a state of sin to that of grace,
than it is to lead a busy, active, zealous
person to the hidden, contemplative
life of the soul.

❈

EXCELLENCE OF THE INTERIOR LIFE

GOD dwelling within us, the life of
CHRIST Himself, when on earth, living
always in His FATHER'S Presence.

It is the life of which S. Paul speaks
when he says, "nevertheless I live;
yet not I. but CHRIST liveth in me."

All saints must lead this life, and their degree of holiness is in proportion to the perfection of their union with GOD.

CHRIST animates their souls, even as the soul animates the body.

They own CHRIST as Master, Counsellor, and Guide; and nothing is done without submitting it to Him, and imploring His aid and approval.

CHRIST is their strength, their refuge, their defender.

They live in constant dependence upon Him, as their Father, Protector, and all-powerful King.

They are drawn to Him, as the child is drawn by love, the poor by need.

They let themselves be guided by Him, as the blind let themselves be led by the child in whom they confide; they bear all suffering that comes from Him, as the sick, in order to be healed, bear suffering at the hands of a physician; and they lean on Him, as the child leans on its mother's breast.

It lifts them above the troubles and miseries of life; the whole world may seem a prey to calamities; themselves, deprived of their goods through injustice or accident; they lose their relations through death, their friends through treachery or forgetfulness, their reputation and honor from slander, a serious illness deprives them of health, their happiness is destroyed by hardness and temptations . . . Ah! no doubt, they will have these trials, no doubt they must shed bitter tears, but still GOD's peace will remain to them, the peace that passeth all understanding; they will realize GOD has ordered it, guided it with His Hand Divine, and they will be able to exclaim with joy, "Thou art left to us, and Thou art all-sufficient!"

Acts of the Interior Life

1. See God, that is to say, be always realizing His Presence, feeling Him near, as the friend from Whom we would never be separated, in work, in prayer, in recreation, in repose. God is not importunate, He never wearies, He is so gracious and merciful, His Hand directs everything, and He will not "suffer us to be tempted above that we are able."

2. Listen to God: be attentive to His counsels, His warnings; we hear His Voice in those Gospel words that recur to our minds, in the good thoughts that suddenly dawn on us, the devout words that meet us in some book, on a sheet of paper, or falling from the lips of a preacher, a friend, or even a stranger.

3. Speak to God: hold converse with Him, more with the heart than the lips, in the early morning's meditation, ejaculatory prayer, vocal prayer, and above all in Holy Communion.

4. *Love God:* be devoted to Him, and Him alone; have no affection apart from Him; restrain the love that would estrange us from Him; *lend* ourselves to all, out of love to Him, but *give* ourselves to Him alone.

5. *Think of God:* reject whatever excludes the thought of Him. Of course, we must fulfil our daily duties, accomplishing them with all the perfection of which we are capable; but they must be done as beneath the Eye of GOD, with the thought that GOD has commanded them, and that to do them carefully is pleasing in His sight.

❈

MEANS BY WHICH TO ATTAIN THE INTERIOR LIFE

1. *Great tenderness of Conscience,* secured by constant, regular, and ear-

nest confession to GOD, a hatred of all sin, imperfection, infidelity, by calmly but resolutely fleeing every occasion of it.

2. *Great purity of heart,* by detachment from all earthly things,—wealth, luxuries, fame, kindred, friends, tastes, even life itself . . . not that we need fail in love to our kindred and friends, but we must only let the thought of them abide in the heart as united to the love and thought of GOD.

3. *Great purity of mind,* carefully excluding from it all useless, distracting thoughts as to past, present, or future; all preoccupation over some pet employment; all desire to be known, and thought well of.

4. *Great purity of action,* only undertaking what lies in the path of duty; controlling natural eagerness and activity; acting soberly, with the help of the HOLY SPIRIT, the thought that by our deeds we glorify GOD;

pausing for a moment, when passing from one occupation to another, in order to direct aright the intention; and taking care to be always occupied in what is useful and beneficial.

5. *Great recollectedness and self-mortification;* avoiding, as much as we can in keeping with our social position, all dissipation, bustle, disturbance; never allowing voluntarily, useless desires, looks, words, or pleasures, but placing them under the rule of reason, decorum, edification, and love; taking care that our prayers be said slowly and carefully, articulating each word, and trying to *feel* the truth of what we are saying.

6. *Great care and exactitude* in all the ordinary actions of life, above all in the exercises of religion: leaving nothing to chance or hazard: beholding in everything GOD's overruling Will, and saying to one's self sometimes, as the hour for such and such

duty arrives, "I must hasten, GOD is calling me."

7. *Much intercourse with God;* speaking to Him with simplicity, loving Him dearly, always consulting Him, rendering to Him an account of every action, thanking Him constantly, and above all, drawing near to Him with joy in the Holy Eucharist. One great help towards such sweet communion with GOD, will be found in a steady perseverance in the early morning's meditation.

8. *Much love for our neighbor,* because he is the much-loved child of GOD, praying for him, comforting, teaching, strengthening, and helping him in all difficulties.

✻

HINDRANCES TO THE INTERIOR LIFE

1. *Natural activity,* always urging us on, and making us too precipitate in all our actions.

It shows itself :—

In our projects, which it multiplies, heaps up, reforms, and upsets. It allows of no rest, until what it has undertaken is accomplished.

In our actions. Activity is absolutely necessary to us. We load ourselves with a thousand things beyond our duty, sometimes even contrary to it. Everything is done with impetuosity and haste, anxiety and impatience to see the end.

In our conversation. Activity makes us speak without thinking, interrupting rudely, reproving hastily, judging without appreciation. We speak loudly, disputing, murmuring, and losing our temper.

In prayer. We burden ourselves with numberless prayers, repeated carelessly, without attention, and with impatience to get to the end of them; it interferes with our meditations, wearies, torments, fatigues the brain, drying up the soul, and hindering the work of the HOLY SPIRIT.

2. *Curiosity* lays the soul open to all external things, fills it with a thousand fancies and questionings, pleasing or vexatious, absorbing the mind, and making it quite impossible to retire within one's self and be recollected. Then follow distaste, sloth, and ennui for all that savors of silence, retirement, and meditation.

Curiosity shows itself, when *studies* are undertaken from vanity, a desire to know all things, and to pass as clever, rather than the real wish to learn in order to be useful—in *reading,* when the spare time is given up to history, papers, and novels—in *walking,* when our steps would lead us where the crowd go to see, to know, only in order to have something to retail; in fact, it manifests itself in a thousand little actions; for instance, pressing forward with feverish haste to open a

letter addressed to us, longing eagerly
to see anything that presents itself,
always being the first to tell any piece
of news. . . . When we forget GOD,
He is driven from the heart, leaving
it void, and then ensues that wild
craving to fill up the void with anything with which we may come into
contact.

3. *Cowardice.* God does not forbid
patient, submissive pleading, but murmuring fears are displeasing to Him,
and He withdraws from the soul that
will not lean on Him. Cowardice
manifests itself when in the *trials of
life* we rebel against the Divine will
that sends us illness, calumny, privation, desertion; when in *dryness of
soul* we leave off our prayers and communions because we feel no sensible
sweetness in them; when we feel a
sickness of the soul that makes us uneasy, and fearful that GOD has forsaken us.

The soul estranged from GOD seeks diversion in the world; but in the midst of the world, GOD is not to be found; when temptations come, wearied, frightened, and tormented, we wander farther and farther away from Him, crying, "I am forsaken," when the trial has really been sent in order to keep us on our guard, prevent our becoming proud, and offering us an opportunity for showing our love.

V.

THE LESSON OF A DAISY

I SAW her from afar, poor child; she looked dreamy as she leaned against the window, and held in her hand a daisy, which she was questioning by gradually pulling it to pieces. What she wanted to ascertain I cannot tell; I only heard in a low murmur, falling from her pale lips, these words: *"a little, a great deal, passionately, not*

at all," as each petal her fingers pulled
away fell fluttering at her feet.

I could see her from a distance, and
I felt touched.

Poor child, why do you tell a flower
the thought that troubles you? have
you no mother?

Why be anxious about the future?
have you not GOD to prepare it for
you, as tenderly as eighteen years ago
your mother prepared your cradle?

Finally, when the daisy was all but
gone, when her fingers stopped at the
last petal, and her lips murmured the
word *little,* she dropped her head upon
her arms, discouraged, and, poor child,
she wept!

❋

Why weep, my child? is it because
this word does not please you?

Let me, let me, in the name of the
simple daisy you have just destroyed,
give you the experience of my old age.

Oh! if you only knew what it costs to have *much* of anything!

A great deal of wit often results in spitefulness which makes us cruel and unjust, in jealousy that torments, in deception that sullies all our triumphs, and pride which is never satisfied.

A great deal of heart causes uneasiness which vexes, pain that rends asunder, grief that nearly kills . . . sometimes even the judgment is deceived.

A great deal of attractiveness means often a consuming vanity, overwhelming deception, an insatiable desire to please, a fear of being unappreciated, a loss of peace, domestic life much neglected.

A great deal of wealth and success is the cause of luxury that enfeebles, loss of calm, quiet happiness, loss of love, leaving only the flattery that captivates.

No, no, my child, never long for

a great deal in this life, unless it be for much forbearance, much goodness.

And if it should be GOD'S Will to give you *much* of anything, then, oh, pray it may never be to your condemnation!

✳

Is *Passionately* the word you long for? Passionately! oh, the harm that is done by that word! there is something in the thought of it that makes me shudder. Passionately means transport, frenzy, excess in everything.

The life that the word *passionately* describes must be a life full of risks and dangers; and if, by little short of a miracle, nothing outwardly wrong appears, the inner life must resemble a palace ravaged by fire, where the stranger sees nothing but cracked walls, blackened furniture, and drapery hanging in shreds.

✳

My child, I would prefer for you the words *not at all,* as applied to fortune, external charms, and all that goes by the name of glory, success, and fascination in the world. I know it may seem a hard sentence, involving a continual self-denial, and exacting incessant hard labor to obtain the bare necessities of life for those we love.

But do not be afraid of it. GOD never leaves His creatures in absolute need. GOD may deprive a face of beauty, a character of amiability, a mind of brilliancy, but He will never take away a heart of love; with the faculty of loving, He adds the power of prayer, and the promise always to listen to and answer it.

As long as we can love and pray, life has charms for us.

Love produces devotion, and devotion brings happiness, even though we may not understand it.

In prayer we feel we are beloved;

and the love of GOD, oh, if only you knew how it compensates for the indifference of our fellow-creatures!

❋

There now only remains to us the last words of the daisy, *a little!* the loving fatherly answer GOD has given to your childish curiosity.

Accept it, and make it the motto of your life!

A little; moderation in wealth and fortune, a condition that promises the most peaceful life, free from anxiety for the future—doubtless requiring daily duties, but permitting many innocent enjoyments.

A little; moderation in our desires, contentment with what we possess, making the most of it, and repressing all vain dreams of a more brilliant position, a more extended reputation, a more famous name.

A little; the affection of a heart devoted to duty, and kindling joy in the family circle, composed of kindred to love, friends to cheer, poor to succor, hearts to strengthen, sufferings to alleviate.

A little; a taste for all that is beautiful,—books, works of art, music, not making us idly dream of fame, but simply providing enjoyment for the mind, all the more keen, as the daily toil renders the occasions rare.

Do you see, my child, how much may lie beneath those simple words, *a little,* that the daisy gave you, and that you seem so much to despise!

Never scorn anything that seems wanting in brilliancy, and remember to be really happy we must have—

More *virtue* than knowledge,
More *love* than tenderness,
More *guidance* than cleverness,
More *health* than riches,
More *repose* than profit.

VI.

EACH day is like a furrow lying before us; our thoughts, desires, and actions are the seed that each minute we drop into it, without seeming to perceive it. The furrow finished, we commence upon another, then another, and again another; each day presents a fresh one, and so on to the end of life . . . sowing, ever sowing. And all we have sown springs up, grows and bears fruit, almost unknown to us; even if by chance we cast a backward glance we fail to recognize our work.

Behind us angels and demons, like gleaners, gather together in sheaves all that belongs to them.

Every night their store is increased. They preserve it, and at the last day will present it to their Master.

Is there not a thought in this that should make us reflect?

VII.

"LEARN OF ME, FOR I AM MEEK AND LOWLY OF HEART"

THIS is a simple rule of life for me, requiring no more than I am able; but I feel it unites me to GOD, makes me more devout, more faithful to duty, more ready for death. Since I have made it my rule, it has been to me a source of consolation, enlightenment, and strength; and yet GOD alone knows how full of pain my life has been!

Dear friends, who, like myself, long to become holy, I commend this sentence to you in all its simplicity; listen, for it comes from the loving Heart of JESUS, it fell from His gentle Lips:—

"Learn of Me, for I am meek and lowly of heart."

I. Be Meek

I. MEEK TOWARDS GOD

LIVING from day to day beneath His Eye, and where all things are ordered by a Divine Providence.

As carefully as a mother arranges the room where her child will pass the day, does GOD prepare each hour that opens before me. Whatever has to be done, it is His Will that I should do it; and in order that it should be done well, He provides the necessary time, intelligence, aptitude, and knowledge.

Whatever of suffering presents itself, He expects me to bear it, even though I may not see any reason for it; and if the pain be so sharp as to call forth a cry, He gently whispers, "Courage, My child, for it is My will!"

If anything occurs to hinder my work, anything goes contrary to my

plans and projects, He has ordained it
so on purpose, because He knows that
too much success would make me
proud, too much ease would make me
sensual; and He would teach me that
the road to heaven is not *success,* but
labor and devotion.

With such thoughts as these all
rebellion is hushed! With what peace,
what joy, our work may be begun,
continued, interrupted, and resumed!

With what energy we reject those
enemies that assail us at every hour,—
idleness, haste, preoccupation, success,
want of perseverance under difficulties!

Does the past sometimes rise up to
trouble me with the thought of the
many years spent without GOD?

Ah! no doubt the shame and grief
are sharp and keen, but why need they
disturb my peace of mind?

Has not GOD promised His pardon
for His blessed SON's sake, to all who

truly repent and unfeignedly believe
His Holy Gospel? Have I made a
full avowal and entire submission? and
am I not willing to fulfil whatever I
am advised in GOD's Name to do for
the future?

Does the future in its turn seem to
frighten me? I smile at the foolish
fancies of my imagination; is not my
future in GOD's Hands?

What, when all that will befall me
to-morrow, next year, ten years,
twenty years hence, is ordained by
Him, shall I distress myself with the
thought that it may not be good for
me!

LORD! be Thou my Guide, and
choose my lot as may seem best to
Thee!

2. MEEK UNDER ALL CIRCUMSTANCES

EVENTS are messengers of either Divine goodness or justice.

Each has a mission to fulfil; and as it comes from GOD, why not let it be accomplished in peace?

Painful, heart-rending, though they may be, they are still the Will of GOD. Watch them as they come, with a little trembling, perhaps even terror, but never let them destroy in the least degree my faith and resignation.

To be meek under these circumstances, does not mean awaiting them with a stoic firmness which proceeds from pride, or hardening one's self against them to the point of repressing all trembling. No! GOD allows us sometimes to anticipate, postpone, or even when possible flee them; at any rate, we may try to soothe and soften them a little.

The GOOD FATHER, when He sends

them, sends at the same time **the** means by which they may be endured, and perhaps averted.

Remedies, in sickness.

Love, in trouble.

Devotion, in privations.

Comfort, in weakness.

Tears, in sorrow.

GOD has created all these; and knowing perhaps that I may fail to find them, He has given commandment to some privileged servants to love, console, soothe, and help me, saying to them,—

"Inasmuch as ye have done it unto one of the least of these My brethren, ye have done it as unto Me."

Oh! welcome then the friendly voice that in the midst of trouble speaks to me of hope; I will receive with gratitude the care that affection presses upon me.

With thankfulness I accept the *time* devoted to me, *privation* borne for my sake; and I will pray GOD to bless these kind friends, and ask Him to say to them words such as these: "All that thou hast done for Mine, I will repay thee a hundred-fold."

3. MEEK TOWARDS OTHERS

THIS may seem even more difficult, for it so often appears to us as if others were actuated by malice.

But how often it is only the result of temperament, pride, thoughtlessness; seeking their own pleasure without a thought of the harm they are doing me; then why be unhappy about it? I need only to be on my guard.

Never stand in the way of others (when it is not the case of a duty to be fulfilled), and if they sometimes are an obstacle in yours, remove them gently, but do not harm them.

Yielding, submitting, retiring, giving up, this should be our conduct towards the members of our family, and those we call our friends.

The more facility you give them for doing what they think right, the more you enter into the feelings they have of their own importance, leaving them a free course of action, so much the more will you be likely to be useful to them, and retain your own peace of mind.

It is astonishing how those we never press open their hearts to us!

Do not try to examine too minutely the actions of others, or the motives that actuate them; if they are wanting in tact, appear not to notice it, or, better still, try to think they have made a mistake.

The best remedy for the dislike we feel towards any one is to endeavor to try to do them a little good every day; the best cure for their dislike to us is to try to speak kindly of them.

Are those around you wicked? be

cautious, but do not lose heart; GOD
will not let them harm you.

How easy for GOD to stay the con-
sequences of slander and calumny!

GOD is the shield, interposing between others, circumstances, and myself.

4. MEEK TOWARDS SELF

THIS does not imply self-compla-
cency, self-indulgence, self-justi-
fication, but simply encouragement,
strength, and fortitude.

Encouragement in some wearisome,
monotonous, unrecognized work, with
a thought like this: "GOD is watching
me, and wishes me to do this." This
labor occupies my mind, perfects my
soul, and shields me from mischief.

Encouragement such as this, in the
midst of sadness and isolation, when
no one thinks of us, or gives us the
smallest token of sympathy, "Is not
my duty sufficient for me? God re-

quires it of me, and it will lead me to heaven."

Strength to rise again after some failure, some humiliating fault, some depressing weakness; rise again lovingly, confidingly, and with the thought, "Never mind, it is a good FATHER, a kind Master, with Whom I have to deal." Confess your sin, humble yourself, and while awaiting the assurance of pardon go on with your daily work with the same zeal as before.

Fortitude against the desertion and forgetfulness of others.

We have two things to fortify us,— *Prayer and Labor.*

One to cheer us,—*Devotion.*

These remedies are always at hand.

II. Be Humble

I. HUMBLE WITH GOD

RESTING always in His presence, like a little child, or even a beggar, who knowing nothing is due to him, still asks, loves, and awaits, feeling sure that hour by hour, in proportion to our need, GOD will provide all that is needful, and even over and above what is absolutely necessary. Live peacefully under the protection of Divine Providence; the more you feel your insignificance, weakness, sickness, misery, the more right you have to the pity and love of GOD.

Only *pray* fervently; let your prayer be thoughtful and reverent, sweet and full of hope. The poor have nothing left to them but *prayer;* but that prayer, so humble, so pleading, ascends to GOD, and is listened to with Fatherly love!

Do not have a number of varied

prayers, but let the "Our Father" be ever on your lips and in your heart.

Love to repeat to God the prayer that Christ Himself has taught, and for His sake is always accepted.

Look upon yourself as a hired servant of God, to whom He has promised a rich reward at the end of the day He calls *life;* each morning hold yourself in readiness to obey all His commands, in the way He wills, and with the means He appoints.

The command may not always come *direct* from the Master; it would be too sweet to hear only God's Voice: but He sends it by means of His ambassadors; these go by the names of *superiors, equals, inferiors,* sometimes *enemies.*

Each has received the mission (without knowing it) to make you holy; one by subduing your independence, another by crushing your pride, a third by spurring your slothfulness.

They will, though fulfilling GOD's command, do it each in his own way, sometimes roughly, sometimes maliciously, sometimes in a way hard to bear . . . what does it matter, so long as you feel that all you do, all you suffer, is the will of GOD?

Do your duty as well as you can, as you understand it, as it is given to you; say sometimes to GOD, "My Master, art Thou satisfied with me?" and then, in spite of ennui, fatigue, repugnance, go on with it faithfully to the end.

Then, whether praise or blame be yours, you will, good faithful servant, at least have peace.

2. HUMBLE TOWARDS OTHERS

LOOK upon yourself as the servant of all, but without ostentation, or their having any knowledge of it.

Repeat to yourself sometimes the

words of the Blessed Virgin Mary:
"Behold the handmaid of the LORD,"
and those of our LORD, "I came not
to be ministered unto, but to minister;"
and then act towards others as if you
were their slave, warning, aiding, lis-
tening; abashed at what they do for
you, and always seeming pleased at
anything they may require you to do
for them.

Oh! if you knew the full meaning
of these words, all they signify of reward in heaven, of joy and peace on
earth, how you would love them!

Oh! if you would only make them
the rule of your life and conduct, how
happy you would be yourself, and
how happy you would make others!

Happy in the approval of con-
sicence, that whispers, "You have done
as CHRIST would have done."

Happy in the thought of the reward
promised to those who give even a cup
of cold water in the name of JESUS

CHRIST; happy in the assurance that GOD will do for you what you have done for others.

Oh! what matters then ingratitude, forgetfulness, contempt, and scorn? They will pain, no doubt, but will have no power to sadden or discourage.

Precious counsel, inspired by CHRIST Himself, I bless you for all the good you have done me!

When first those words found entrance to my heart, they brought with them *peace* and *strength* to stand against *deception, desertion, discouragement* and the *resolute will* to live a life more devoted to GOD, more united to Him, more contented, and ever pressing onward towards heaven. Once more, I bless you!

Precious counsels, enlighten, guide, and lead me.

VIII.

A Simple Prayer

O JESU! in the midst of glory forget not the sadness upon earth!

Have mercy upon those to whom God has sent the bitter trial of separation from those they love!

Have mercy on that loneliness of heart, so full of sadness, so crushing, sometimes full of terror!

Have mercy upon those struggling against the difficulties of life, and faint with discouragement!

Have mercy on those whom fortune favors, whom the world fascinates, and who are free from care!

Have mercy on those to whom Thou hast given great tenderness of heart, great sensitiveness!

Have mercy on those who cease to love us, and never may they know the pain they cause!

Have mercy on those who have gradually withdrawn from Holy Communion and Prayer, and losing peace within, weep, yet dare not return to Thee!

Have mercy on all we love; make them holy even through suffering! if ever they estrange themselves from Thee, take, oh, take all my joys, and decoy them with the pleasures back again to Thee!

Have mercy on those who weep, those who pray, those who know not *how* to pray!

To all, O Jesus, grant Hope and Peace!

IX.

Simple Counsels for a Young Girl

YES, very simple. Listen my child, and may they sink deep into your heart, as the dew sinks in the calyx of the flower.

These are my counsels:—

Distrust the love that comes too suddenly.

Distrust the pleasure that fascinates so keenly.

Distrust the words that trouble or charm.

Distrust the book that makes you dream.

Distrust the thought you cannot confide to your mother.

Treasure these counsels, and sometimes as you read them, ask yourself, *"Why?"* Guardian Angel of the child we are addressing, teach her the reason of these sentences that seem to her so exaggerated!

X.

A RECIPE FOR NEVER ANNOYING OUR FRIENDS

THIS was made by one who had suffered much for many years from numberless little worries, occasioned by a relative, whose affection no doubt was sincere and devoted, but also too ardent, and wanting in discretion.

There must be moderation in all things, even in the love we manifest, the care we take to shield them from trouble.

This recipe consists of but four simple rules, very clear, very precise. Behold them:—

1. *Always leave my friend something more to desire of me.* If he asks me to go and see him three times, I go but twice. He will look forward to my coming a third time, and when I go, receive me the more cordially.

It is so sweet to feel we are needed, and so hard to be thought importunate.

2. *Be useful to my friend as far as he permits, and no farther.*

An over-anxious affection becomes tiresome, and a multiplicity of beautiful sentiments makes them almost insupportable.

Devotion to a friend does not consist in doing *everything* for him, but simply that which is agreeable and of service to him, and let it only be revealed to him by accident.

We all love freedom, and cling tenaciously to our little fancies; we do not like others to arrange what we have purposely left in disorder; we even resent their over-anxiety and care for us.

3. *Be much occupied with my own affairs, and little, very little, with those of my friend.*

This infallibly leads to a favorable result. To begin with, in occupying myself with my own affairs, I shall the more speedily accomplish them, while my friend is doing the same.

If he appeals to me for help, I will go through fire and water to serve him, but if *not,* then I do both myself and

him the greater service by abstaining.
If, however, I can serve him without
his knowledge of it, and I can see his
need, then I must be always ready to
do it.

4. *Leave my friend always at liberty
to think and act for himself in matters
of little importance.* Why compel him
to think and act with me? Am *I* the
type of all that is beautiful and right?
Is it not absurd to think that because
another acts and thinks differently to
myself, he must needs be wrong? No
doubt I may not always say, *"You are
right,"* but I can at any rate let him
think it.

Try this recipe of mine, and I can
answer for it your friendship will be
lasting.

XI.

BENEATH THE EYE OF GOD, GOD ONLY

AS you read these words, are you not conscious of an inward feeling of peace and quietness?

Beneath God's Eye! there is something in the thought like a sheltering rock, a refreshing dew, a gleam of light.

Ah! why always such seeking for some one to *see* me, to *understand, appreciate, praise* me?

The human eye I seek is like the scorching ray that destroys all the delicate colors in the most costly material. Every action that is done, only to be seen of others, loses its freshness in the sight of GOD, like the flower that passing through many hands is at last hardly presentable.

Oh, my soul! be as the desert flower that grows. blooms. and flourishes unseen, in obedience to GOD's Will, and cares not whether the passing bird perceives it, or the wind scatters the petals, scarcely formed.

＊

On no account neglect the duty you owe to friendship, relatives, society, but remember each day to reserve some portion of it for yourself and GOD only.

Remember always to do some actions that can be known to none but GOD.

Ah! how sweet to have GOD as our only Witness.

It is the high degree of holiness.

The most exquisite happiness.

The assurance of an entry into heaven hereafter.

The mother that reserves all that is most costly for her child, the child that prepares in secret some surprise for its mother, do not experience a joy more pure, more elevating, than the servant of GOD, who lives always in GOD's Presence, Whom alone they would please, or the loving heart that enclosing alms to some destitute family writes upon the cover these words only, "In the name of the Good and Gracious GOD."

❉

The following lines were found on some scraps of paper belonging to some stranger: . . . They have just told me of a poor destitute woman; I gave them ten pence for her; it was my duty to set an example. And now, my GOD, for Thee, for Thy sake only, I mean to send her five shillings, which I shall deduct from my personal expenses.

. . . To-morrow Henry is coming to see me, that poor Henry I loved so dearly, but who has grown cold towards his old friend. He wished to grieve me, and little knows that I found it out. Help me, LORD, to remember I have forgiven him, and help me to receive him cordially.

Thou alone knowest all I have suffered.

. . . What a happy day was yesterday! happy with regard to heavenly things, for alas! my poor heart suffered.

Yesterday was a festival. The snow outside kept every one at home by their own firesides, and I was left lonely . . . Ah, yes, my heart felt sad, but my spirit was peaceful; I tried to talk to GOD, just as if I could really see Him at my side, and gradually I felt comforted, and spent my evening with a sweet sense of GOD'S Presence.

. . . What I said, what I wrote, I know not; but the remembrance of yesterday remains to me as some sweet, refreshing perfume.

✱

Perhaps at the Last Day all that will remain worth recording of a life full of activity and zeal will be those little deeds that were done solely beneath the Eye of GOD. . . .

My GOD, teach me to live with an abiding sense of Thy Presence, laboring for Thee, suffering for Thee, guided by Thee, . . . and Thee alone!

XII.

MY DUTY TOWARDS GOD

PRAYERS.

Slow, recollected, persevering.

Peaceful, calm, resigned.

Simple, humble, trusting.

Always reverent, as loving as possible.

Charitable. Have I not always opportunity to give? to thank?

SUBMISSION.

To my lot and to my duty: they come from GOD, are ordained by GOD, lead me to GOD, to neglect them is to estrange myself from Him.

To the Guide of my soul: He has received the Holy Spirit in order to show me the way; he has GOD'S Spirit to guide him.

To my Parents: they have GOD'S authority.

To circumstances: they are arranged and sent by GOD.

LABOR.

Begun cheerfully.
Continued perseveringly.
Interrupted and resumed patiently.
Finished perfectly and devoutly.

Repose and care for the body, as in GOD's Sight, under GOD's protection.

DUTY TOWARDS MY NEIGHBOR

GOOD EXAMPLE.

By modest demeanor and simple dress.
By a smiling face and pleasing manner.
Always striving to give pleasure.
Faithfully fulfilling every duty.

GOOD WORDS.

Zealous without affectation, encouraging, consoling, peaceful, joyful, loving. These are possible every day.

GOOD DEEDS.

Service rendered by alms, by industry, by influence.

Ills remedied, by excusing, justify-
ing, protecting, defending, con-
cealing faults and mistakes; if
possible, by repairing them.

Joys provided, for the *mind,* by a
joyous manner; for the *heart,* by
loving thanks; for the soul, by a
word of Heaven.

My Duty Towards Myself

COURAGE.

In trials and adversity, disturbance,
sickness, failure, humiliations.

Worries that trouble without reason.

Ill temper controlled, in order not to
pain others.

After failures, to begin again.

In temptations, to withstand them.

ORDER AND METHOD.

In my occupation, each at its appointed hour.

In my recreation.

In all material things, for my benefit.

Shunning scruples and constraint as much as caprice and folly.

NOURISHMENT.

Pious thoughts, read, meditated upon, and sometimes written.

Books that elevate and excite love for all that is good and lovely.

Conversations that refresh, rejoice, and cheer; walks that expand the mind, as well as strengthen the body.

XIII.

THE POWER OF AN ACT OF LOVE TO-WARDS GOD

HAVE you ever reflected upon this? Let us consider the exact words that describe it.

"I love Thee with all my heart, with all my soul, with all my strength, because Thou art so good, so infinitely good!"

Try and repeat these words slowly,

so that each may penetrate deep into your heart.

Do you not feel moved, as if your whole being in these words went forth to GOD, offering to Him life itself?

Do you not feel, in making this Act of Love, you give far more than if you gave your wealth, influence, or time; nay, rather does not this very act seem to bring you riches, strength, opportunities, all that you possess?

Picture to yourself, standing before you, a child—a child perhaps who may have injured you deeply, and yet whose sincerity at this moment you cannot doubt, who is actuated neither by fear nor self-seeking, but simply by a penitent heart, and who comes to say to you words of love, such as those above, do you feel no emotion, no feeling of pity?

I defy you to be without some emotion, not to feel your arms extending, perhaps in spite of you, to embrace this poor child, and not to answer, *"I also love thee."*

I have yet another test to put to you, poor, desolate, guilty, hopeless as you are, seeing only within and around you, *fears, terror,* and—ay, let me say it—*damnation.*

I defy you to kneel and say these words (laying a greater stress on them because of the repugnance you feel): *"My God! I love Thee with all my heart, with all my strength, with all my soul, above everything, because Thou art so good, so infinitely good!"* and then not to feel that JESUS is moved with compassion, and not to hear His Voice, saying to you, "My child, I love thee also!"

O JESUS, how can we find words in which to express the tenderness awakened in Thine Heart, by a word of love from one of Thy little ones? That Heart, so tender, gentle, sensitive, and loving!

A sentence of Faber's may sound unnatural to us, so little spiritually minded: he says, "GOD sometimes draws us to Him, and fills us with love for Him, not that He may love us, *that* He always does, but in order to make us *feel* how He loves us!"

An Act of Love demands but a few moments. The whole of the day, even in the midst of labor, we can multiply it infinitely, and what wonders are wrought by each Act!

JESUS Himself is glorified, and He sheds abundant grace upon the earth.

Our Guardian Angel, beholding us, listens, draws nearer, and makes us feel we have done right.

The Angels above experience a sudden joy, and look upon us tenderly.

Evil spirits feel their power diminished, and there is a moment of rest from the temptation that surrounds us.

The choir of saints above renew their songs of praise.

Each soul on earth feels the peace Divine.

Ah! which of us each day would not renew these Acts of Love to GOD!

Ah! all who read these lines, pause for one moment, and from the bottom of your heart exclaim, "My GOD, I love Thee! My GOD, I love Thee!"

XIV.

BE SERIOUS

A STATESMAN retiring from public life occupied himself in his latter days with serious thoughts.

The friends who came to visit him, reproached him with being melancholy. "No," he replied; "I am only *serious*. All around me is serious, and I feel the need that heart and mind should be in unison with my surroundings.

"For," he added, with such solemnity as to impress all present, "GOD is *serious* as He watches us. JESUS is *serious* when He intercedes for us. The HOLY SPIRIT is *serious* when He guides us. Satan is *serious* when he tempts us. The wicked in hell are *serious* now, because they neglected to be so when on earth; all is *serious* in that world whither we are wending."

Oh, my friends! believe me, it is all true; let us at least at times be *serious* in our thoughts and in our actions.

XV.

CONSOLATION

YOU distress yourself sometimes, poor thing! because amongst those who surround you, there are one or two who worry and annoy you. They do not like you, find fault with everything you do, they meet you with a severe countenance and austere manner, you think they do you harm, you look upon them as obstacles to your doing good.

Your life passes away saddened and faded, and gradually you become disheartened. Courage! instead of vexing yourself, thank GOD; these very persons are the means of preserving you from humiliating faults, perhaps even greater sins.

It is like the blister the doctor applies, to draw out the inflammation that would kill.

GOD sees that too much joy, too much happiness, procured by those little attentions for which you are so eager, would make you careless and slothful in prayer; too much affection would only enervate, and you would cling too much to earthly things; so in order to preserve your heart in all its tenderness and simplicity, He plants there a few thorns, and cuts you off from all the pleasures you fancy yours by right. GOD knows that too much praise would cause pride, and make you less forbearing to others,

and so He sends instead humiliations.
Let them be, then, these persons who
unconsciously are doing GOD'S work
within you.

If you cannot love them from sympathy, love with an effort of the will,
and say to GOD, "My GOD, grant that
without offending Thee, they may
work my sanctification. I have need
of them."

XVI.

HOLY COMMUNION

THE result of a good Communion
is, *within,* a fear of a sin, *without,* a love for others.

Holy Communion is a great aid to
sanctification.

JESUS visits the soul, working in it,
and filling it with His Grace, which is
shed on all around, as the sun sheds
forth its light, the fire gives out its
heat.

It is impossible but that CHRIST,

thus visiting the soul, should not leave
something CHRIST-like within, if only
the soul be disposed to receive it.
Fire, whose property is to give
warmth, cannot produce that effect
unless the body be placed near enough
to be penetrated with the heat.

Does not this simple thought explain
the reason that there is often so little
result from our frequent Communions?

Do you long at each Communion to
receive the grace bestowed by CHRIST
that shall little by little fit you for
heaven hereafter?

Will you, receiving thus the GOD of
Peace within, have for those around
you kind words that shall fill them with
calmness, resignation, and peace?

Will you, receiving thus the GOD of
Love, gradually increase in tenderness
and love that will urge you to sacrifice
yourself for others, loving them as
CHRIST would have loved them?

Will you, receiving Him you rightly name the *Gracious* GOD, become yourself gracious, gracious to sympathize, gracious to forbear, gracious to pardon, and thus in a small way resemble the GOD Who gave Himself for thee?

This should be your resolve when about to communicate.

Resolved: to obey GOD's Commandments in all their extensiveness, never hesitating in a question of duty, no matter how hard it may be; the duty of forgiving and forgetting some injustice or undeserved rebuke; accepting cheerfully a position contrary to your wishes and inclinations; application to some labor, distasteful, and seemingly beyond your strength. . . .

If your duty seems almost *impossible* to fulfil, ask yourself, "Is this GOD's Will for me?" and if conscience answers *yes,* then reply also, *I will do it.*

All difficulties vanish after Holy Communion.

Generous: depriving yourself those days of Communion of some pleasures which though harmless in themselves, you know, only too well, enfeeble your devotion, excite your feelings, and leave you weaker than before. *Generous* means doing over and above what duty requires of us.

Conscientious and upright: not seeking to find out if some forbidden thing is really a *sin* or not, and whether it may not in some way be reconciled to conscience.

Oh! how hurtful are these waverings between GOD and the world, duty and pleasure, obedience and allurements. Did JESUS CHRIST hesitate to die for you? and yet *you* hesitate! Coward!

Humble and meek: treading peacefully the road marked out for you by Providence, sometimes weeping, often suffering, but free from anxiety, awaiting the loving support that never fails those who trust and renew their strength day by day. Living quietly, loving neither the world nor its praise, working contentedly in that state of life to which you are called, doing good, regardless of man's knowledge and approval, content that others should be more honored, more esteemed, having only one ambition,— *to love God, and be loved by Him.*

❋

If this be the disposition of your soul, then be sure each Communion will be blessed to you, make you more holy, more like CHRIST, with more taste and love for the things of GOD, more sure of glory hereafter.

XVII.

AFTER HOLY COMMUNION

SELF-SACRIFICE

LORD! take me and lead me whithersoever Thou willest! Is it Thy Will that my life be spent in the midst of such incessant toil and tumult that no time is left for those brief moments of leisure of which I sometimes dream?

Yes! yes! I wish it also!

Is it Thy Will that lonely and sorrowful I am left on earth, while those I loved have gone to dwell near Thee above?

Yes! yes! I wish it also!

Is it Thy Will that unknown by all, misunderstood even by those whose affection I prize, I am looked upon as useless, on account of my stupidity, want of manner, or bad health?

Yes! yes! I wish it also!

Thou art Ruler. O my GOD! only

be Thyself the Guide, and abide with
me forever!

MY MEMORY

MY Memory! the mysterious book
—reflection of that of eternity,
in which at each moment are inscribed
my thoughts, affections, and desires.

Into Thy Hands I commend it,
LORD, that Thou alone mayst write
there, Thou alone efface!

Leave there, LORD, the remembrance
of my sins, but efface forever the
pleasures that led to them—were I to
catch but a glimpse of their enticing
sweetness, I might again desire them.
Leave there the sweet memories of
childhood, when I loved Thee with
such simplicity, and my father, my
mother, my family, were my sole affections. Those days, when the slightest
untruthfulness, or even the fear of
having sinned, left me no peace till I
had confessed it to my mother. Those

days, when I always felt my Guardian
Angel near me, helping me in my
work, and soothing my little troubles!

Leave me the remembrance of my
first sense of the Divine absolution,
when my heart overflowing with secret
joy, I cried, *I am forgiven, I am forgiven!*

And then the recollection of my first
Communion! oh, recall it to me, LORD,
with its preparation so fearful, yet so
loving; its joy so calm, so holy, yet
so sweet, that even now the thought
of it fills mine eyes with tears!

Leave me the remembrance of Thy
Benefits! each year of my life is
crowned with blessings . . . at *ten* . . .
fifteen . . . *eighteen* . . . *twenty* years
. . . oh! I can well recall all Thy
goodness to me, my GOD! Yes, receive
my memory, blot out all that can estrange me from Thee, and grant that
nothing apart from Thee may again
find a place there!

MY MIND

OH! by what false lights have I
been dazzled! They showed me
prayer as wearisome; religious duties
too absorbing; frequent Communion
as useless; social duties as a heavy
bondage; devotion the lot of weak
minds and those without affection . . .
Oh, I knew well how false it was, and
yet I let myself be half-convinced!

When have I ever been more *zealous
in labor* than those days when I had
fulfilled all my religious duties?

When more *loving and devoted* than
on the days of my Communions?

When have I felt *more free, more
happy,* than when having fulfilled all
the duties of my social position?

LORD, receive my mind, and nourish
it with Thy Truth!

Show me that apart from Thee,
pleasures of the senses leave behind

only remorse, disgust, weariness, and satiety.

Pleasures of the heart cause anxiety, bitterness, rendings, and fears.

Pleasures of the mind produce a void, vanity, jealousy, coldness, and humiliations! Teach me that all must pass away . . . that nothing is true, nothing is good, nothing is eternal, but Thou, Thou only, O my GOD!

MY WILL

MY deeds are the result of my will, and it is the will only that makes them of any value. Oh, then to begin with, I will learn submission! What I *wish,* may not always be good for me; what I am *bidden* must be right.

O JESUS! grant me the grace of *obedience,* and then let me be bidden many things: works of piety, works of charity, self-renunciation. brilliant deeds, deeds that are ignored in my family life, or wherever I may be, there are numberless calls for all of these; LORD, behold Thy servant! may I be always ready when Thou hast need of me!

ALL THAT I HAVE

MY GOD, how richly hast Thou blessed me!

Treasures of love, I offer them to Thee!

I have relations, dear ones, Thou knowest how I love them. . . . Ah, if it be Thy Will to take them from this world, before me, though I say it weeping, still I say it, Thy Will be done!

I have friends. . . . If it be Thy Will they should forget me, think ill of me, leave me alone, with that loneliness of heart so bitter and so keen . . . I yield them to Thee!

I have worldly goods that give me a certain degree of comfort, by affording me the means of helping others poorer than myself. . . . Should it be Thy Will to deprive me of them, little by little, till at last I have only the bare necessaries of life left . . . I yield them to Thee!

I have limbs that Thou hast given me. If it be Thy Will that paralysis should fetter my arms, my eyes no longer see the light, my tongue be unable to articulate, my GOD, I yield them to Thee!

In exchange, grant me Thy Love, Thy Grace, and then . . . nothing more, only Heaven!

✳

O JESUS, abandoned by all in the garden of Gethsemane, in need then of comfort and strength:

JESUS, Thou Who knowest that at this moment there are some on earth who have no strength, no comfort, no support, oh! send to them some angel who will give them a little joy, a little peace! Oh, if only *I* might be that messenger! What must I suffer, LORD?

If an outward trouble or inward pain be needful to make of me but for one moment a consoling angel to some poor lonely heart, oh! however keen the pain, or bitter the trouble, I pray Thee, grant it to me, JESUS!

O JESUS, in search of *lips* to tell the love Thou bearest for Thy children; *lips* to tell the poor and lonely they are not despised, the sinful they are not cast away, the timid they are not unprotected. O JESUS! grant that my lips may speak words of strength, love, comfort, and pardon. Let each day seem to me wasted that passes without my having spoken of help and sympathy, without having made some one bless Thy Name, be it but a little child.

O JESUS! so *patient* towards those who wearied Thee with their importunity and ignorance! JESUS, so long-suffering in teaching, and awaiting the hour of grace! JESUS, grant that I may be patient to listen, to teach, though over and over again I may have to instruct the same thing. Grant me help, that I may always show a smiling face, even though the importunity of some be keenly felt! and if through physical weakness I manifest ennui or weariness, grant, O JESUS, that I may speedily make amends, with loving words, for the pain I have caused.

O JESUS! Who with infinite tact didst await, seated at the roadside, the opportunity for doing good, simply asking a small service of the poor Samaritan woman Thou wouldst save, and draw to Thee.

O JESUS! grant that I may feel and understand all the pain that timidity, shyness, or reserve keep buried within the recesses of the soul. Grant me the tact and discretion that draws near without paining, that asks without repulsing, without humiliating, and thus enable me to bring peace and comfort to the wounded heart.

O JESUS! seeking some one as faithful dispenser of Thy blessings, grant *much* to me, that I may have much to bestow on others. Grant that my hands may dispense Thine alms, that they may be as Thine, when Thou didst wash the feet of Thine Apostles, working for all, helping all; let me never forget that, like Thee, I am placed on this earth to minister, not to be ministered unto.

Grant that my lips may speak comforting words and give forth cheering smiles, that I may be as the well by the roadside, where the weary traveller stoops to drink, as the shade of the tree whose branches laden with fruit are extended over all that pass beneath.

O JESUS! to Whom all Thy children are so dear, and whatever they may be Thou carest for them, and rememberest they are the much-loved children of GOD! Oh! grant that in all my intercourse with others, I may only see, love, and care for their *souls,* that soul for whom, O GOD, Thou hast died, who like myself can call Thee FATHER, and with whom, near Thee, I hope to dwell, throughout the ages of Eternity.